Making Waves

10 years of the Byron Bay Writers Festival

Edited by Marele Day,
Susan Bradley Smith and Fay Knight

First published 2006 by University of Queensland Press
PO Box 6042, St Lucia, Queensland 4067 Australia

www.uqp.uq.edu.au

This collection © Northern Rivers Writers' Centre 2006
Contributions © individual authors 2006

This book is copyright. Except for private study, research, criticism or reviews, as permitted under the Copyright Act, no part of this book may be reproduced, stored in a retrieval system, or transmitted in any form or by any means without prior written permission. Enquiries should be made to the publisher.

Typeset by Post Pre-press Group, Brisbane
Printed in Australia by McPherson's Printing Group

Cataloguing in Publication Data
National Library of Australia

Day, Marele.
  Making waves: 10 years of the Byron Bay Writers Festival.

  ISBN 0 7022 3583 0.

  1. Byron Bay Writers Festival. 2. Authors, Australian – New South Wales – Byron Bay. 3. Authors, Australian – 20th century. 4. Authors, Australian – 21st century. 5. Festivals – New South Wales – Byron Bay. I. Knight, Fay, 1955– . II. Bradley Smith, Susan. III. Title.

808.02099443

Making
Waves

CONTENTS

INTRODUCTION Marele Day, Susan Bradley Smith,
  Fay Knight ... vii
KATE GRENVILLE *Saying the Unsayable* ... 1
HILARY McPHEE *The Hunger for Good Talk* ... 10
PETER GOLDSWORTHY *Travels with My Inner Toad* ... 16
DOROTHY PORTER *Numbers* ... 23
RUTH OSTROW *The Violin* ... 25
NICK EARLS *Men at Work* ... 29
JEAN BEDFORD *The Woman on the Train* ... 35
MUNGO MacCALLUM *The Best Weekend of the Year* ... 40
SUSAN BRADLEY SMITH *The Long Grass of Talent:
  David Williamson in Interview* ... 45
LARRY BUTTROSE *After Theory* ... 56
ANITA HEISS *Aboriginal Writers on the Significance
  of Space, Sense of Place and Connection to Country* ... 67
JOHN KINSELLA *Line Breaks and Back-Draft:
  Not a Defence of a Poem* ... 84
JOHN CARROLL *Universal Rights – Singular Culture:
  On the Clash of Civilisations* ... 96

PETER CORRIS *The Big Burn*	106
DAVID LESER *Helen Garner and the Agony of Writing*	111
ALISON BROINOWSKI *This Is the Way the World Ends*	128
ROBYN WILLIAMS *Not in Flagrante Delicto?*	147
MELISSA LUCASHENKO *Essays and the New Journalism*	151
PETER SINGER *The Ethical Responsibilities of Writers Addressing Political Issues*	155
CHRISTOPHER KREMMER *American Empire: Politics and Culture in the 21st Century*	163
ROGER McDONALD *The Slim Find*	174
CRAIG McGREGOR *Blood and the Nation*	193
DI MORRISSEY *Talking Up a Festival*	212
THEA ASTLEY *Why I Wrote a Short Story Called 'Diesel Epiphany'*	222
Contributors	227
Editors	235
Acknowledgments	237
Endnotes	239

INTRODUCTION

A festival doesn't simply manifest: it starts with a wish list, a plan of the elements involved, a mapping out of the terrain. Like a work of architecture, it is conceived first in the mind. Ten years ago a small group of locals led by Chris Hanley, president of the Northern Rivers Writers' Centre, had the idea of a writers festival for Byron Bay. It was a big vision with no guarantee of materialising. Situated in the subtropical latitudes of northern New South Wales, Byron was better known for surf and laid-back lifestyle. Would invited writers come, and, more to the point, would there be an audience? That first year, 1997, in the Byron Bay Beach Resort, there were fifty writers and a small but committed audience. Ten years later people still come to Byron for the surf, but the Festival itself is making waves with 100 writers, five on-site venues, and an audience of more than 40,000. As Robyn Williams says, 'Byron stands for something – artistic freedom, creativity and openness to ideas. And Byron means weather.'

At a time when dissension can be read as sedition, and

free expression is increasingly under threat nationally and internationally, the confluence of ideas, words, opinions and people which a writers festival represents is vital.

This anthology is a celebration of what the Byron Bay Writers Festival has become, its independence, its particular flavour, and the forum it provides for intelligent discussion. Hilary McPhee points out that 'we need all the opportunities for public and private exchange we can get'. Like the Festival itself, the anthology began with an idea, the drawing up of a wish list, a planning of the elements involved.

Writers who have been guests and supporters of the Festival were invited to address the 'big issues', the things that mattered to them as writers and as Australians. While most of the contributions are in essay form, writers also presented short stories, a poem. We don't necessarily endorse all of the views expressed herein, but we fully support the right to express them, and in whatever form the writer chooses.

In the ensemble the contributions engage in dialogue with each other, talking among themselves. A phrase or an idea brought to life in one piece echoes through others. They are in turn insightful, thought-provoking, heart-felt, poignant, witty.

Kate Grenville begins by evoking the power of language, particularly the language of fiction. Melissa Lucashenko writes from an Indigenous point of view, encouraging fellow writers to keep going, even when their words fall on deaf ears, and Peter Singer urges writers to follow the argument where it leads.

We discovered that what mattered to the writers was both the political and the personal. John Carroll, Alison Broinowski and Christopher Kremmer address global concerns and the shadow cast on them by the spectre of America. Larry Buttrose questions the validity of theory for contemporary writers, while

David Williamson, in an interview with Susan Bradley Smith, reveals his collision with it.

Peter Goldsworthy casts the Internet as a collective Id of our anxieties and obsessions. Dorothy Porter prefers mystery to the cut-and-dried perfection of numbers and John Kinsella breaks apart the line break.

Anita Heiss takes us on a journey around Indigenous Australia, showing us the country beneath the concrete. A palpable sense of place, our relationship to it and each other, is continued in the stories by Roger McDonald and Craig McGregor.

Moving to the personal, David Leser presents a revealing portrait of Helen Garner, Jean Bedford imagines a life for a woman on a train, Nick Earls reflects on the perils of house-sharing. Ruth Ostrow connects to her deceased father, and Peter Corris ponders the dubious catharsis of losing one's possessions in a house fire.

Mungo MacCallum and Di Morrissey give us an insider's view of the Festival itself, the atmosphere of the fairground as well as what happens in the tents.

And finally, Thea Astley. What better way to end the anthology than with her last public performance, at the Byron Bay Writers Festival in 2004, and its final word – Ah.

In assembling this anthology we would like to thank the writers themselves for their generosity, Jill Eddington, the indefatigable director of the Festival who smoothed the way, and our publisher, UQP, which has brought this festival on the page into print.

Marele Day
Susan Bradley Smith
Fay Knight

KATE GRENVILLE
Saying the Unsayable

Kate appeared at the very first Byron Bay Writers Festival in 1997 and delivered this inaugural Thea Astley lecture at the Festival in 2005.

Thea Astley was one of our truly original writers. Many great contributors to Australian life had to wait until they were dead before they were given the recognition they deserved, but Thea was, remarkably and wonderfully, not one of them. She had the satisfaction of knowing in her own lifetime that she'd spoken to a whole generation – several generations – of Australians and helped to shape our idea of ourselves.

Her spirit is definitely here with us today: fag sending up smoke signals, sunnies hiding her eyes, that knowing smile. And behind the smile, that brain – as sharp as the crease in a Frenchman's jeans.

She had an unerring bullshit detector. In preparing for this lecture, various high-flown grandiose themes were coming to mind. Large pronouncements were readying themselves on the subject of 'The Uses of History' and 'Whither Fiction?' Fortunately, Thea was listening, and was kind enough to send a little message along. This was what she told me, through the medium of page 148 of *It's Raining in Mango*: 'The inky voice of the speaker was processing all the permutations of the banal. But the crowd of listeners, instead of fidgeting, of growing restless, was riveted on the pulpy face and goldfish mouth through which these plangent nothings pumped.' Hearing you loud and clear, Thea.

The first book of Thea's I read was *A Kindness Cup*, which was published in 1974. Re-reading it recently I was awed at how ahead of her time she was. Thirty years ago she knew what some of us are only just waking up to: the fact that our own history provides a powerful engine for fiction, and that the voice of fiction can say the unspoken about that history. What I'm going to talk about today is something about the place where history and language meet, and what goes on there.

The received wisdom about Australian history when I was growing up was that basically we didn't have any. The best we could come up with were the explorers, doggedly dying in search of that Inland Sea, the convicts, the gold rushes. The invention of the stump-jump plough seemed to be one of the highlights of our achievements. Unlike those lucky other countries such as Britain, we'd had no real history: no kings and queens, no invasions, no wars.

Except that we did, of course. We'd had an invasion, and we'd had a war that lasted a hundred years or so. But by a sleight of hand of semantics, it was possible to erase those events from the record, just by calling them by other names. We called the invasion of Australia by Europeans 'discovery' and 'settlement' and we called the guerrilla war waged by the Aboriginal people 'attacks'. (Nineteenth-century newspapers quaintly called that war 'outrages and depredations by our sable brethren'.) By doing nothing more than choosing one set of words over another, and making sure they were bland and boring words, we'd concealed what happened with amazing effectiveness.

Researching early Australian history recently, I became more and more interested not only in the events but in the voice used to record them, and what that voice did to the events.

One of the incidents that caught my ear was an account of the first punitive raid against the Aboriginal people, in December 1790. The governor's gamekeeper was speared to death and the governor decided to retaliate. Here – edited for brevity – is how he described what he thought should happen.

> The Governor, in order to deter the natives from such practices in future, has ordered out a party to search for the man who wounded the convict in such a dangerous manner on Friday last . . . in order to make a signal example of that tribe . . .
>
> A party consisting of 2 captains, 2 subalterns, and 40 privates from the garrison (with a proper number of non-commissioned officers), with three days' provisions, is to be ready to go out tomorrow morning at daylight, in order to bring in six of those natives who reside near the head of Botany Bay, or if that should be found impracticable, to put that number to death.

This is better than the stump-jump plough. It's pretty dramatic stuff. But look at how hard the governor has worked to leach the interest out of it. That last paragraph lulls the reader into somnolence with its punctilious enumerations: the captains, the subalterns, the privates – with a proper number of non-commissioned officers, of course – the provisions, the leaving at daylight. It sounds like the dullest kind of school camp.

Even when it gets to the point, the language is as impersonal and uninteresting as possible. The men are to 'bring in' the natives. They might bring in the washing while they're there, too. And what about that word 'impracticable': 'to bring in six of those natives . . . or if that should be found impracticable, to put that number to death'. Such a reasonable little word – a sensible shoes and cardigan sort of word. How can you argue with it? And the point to which all this leads – just an afterthought really: 'or . . . to put that number to death'. To put to death – how beautifully impersonal this is, in its passive voice, and what a fine quasi-legal loftiness it has. Somewhere embedded in that phrase 'to put to death' is the suggestion that such a killing is justified, the way an execution could be considered justified – it's sad, but necessary, even inevitable.

But beyond these bland words, think of the pictures. Some fifty armed men are going to go to the head of Botany Bay and are going to capture six Aboriginal men. There's no way of identifying the one who speared the gamekeeper, so any ones will do.

The soldiers would have had to try to surround them, perhaps chase them through the bush: fifty soldiers galumphing through the bush with their three days' provisions bumping up and down on their backs. Once they caught the men, they'd have had to tie them up. Imagine it: at least two men would have to hold each Aboriginal man while another couple of men got the ropes around him. To get the job done, the soldiers would have to more or less embrace the black men. There would have been biting and clawing, violence eyeball to eyeball.

But if that didn't work – wasn't 'practicable' – the soldiers would have to kill them. Shooting from a distance, with those hopeless old muskets, would have only winged them at best. In order to 'put them to death', the soldiers would have had to come in close and shoot again at point-blank range. That meant they'd have to shoot wounded men who were lying on the ground looking up at them. Even then, they wouldn't all die instantly. The soldiers would have to watch, and listen, as the six Aboriginal men died more or less slowly. That was the reality behind those calm little words 'are to be put to death'.

The language the governor uses is also an amazing achievement of smoke and mirrors mathematically. The soldiers are to go out, at the start of the extract, 'to search for the man who wounded the convict' – that is, one man. By the end of that same sentence the aim is to 'make an example of the tribe' – the whole lot of them. Specifically, by the end of the statement, six people are to be brought in. All that fine language fudges the reality, which was that one dead European was considered to be worth six dead 'natives'.

Watkin Tench was the captain put in charge of this operation, and he left his own account of his orders. Only this chance fact allows us to know the even more horrific reality behind the governor's orders.

Tench tells us that he was to go to Botany Bay and so on as above: 'we were, if practicable, to bring away two natives as prisoners and to put to death ten'. He haggled with the governor and got that number reduced to six, as in the official order. Then, quite casually, he tells us something the governor hadn't thought to mention in his official account: after killing the men, Tench says, 'we were to cut off and bring in the heads of the slain: for which purpose hatchets and bags would be furnished'.

Again, this language is masterly in its ability to make a moment of high drama about as interesting as the instructions that come with the toaster. Scrupulously grammatical: 'for which purpose'. Splendidly bland: 'cut off and bring in'. Exquisitely impersonal: no one was actually furnishing the bags, it was just that, in the passive voice, they 'would be furnished'. It's the language of a good quartermaster, making sure the troops have everything they need. Socks, food, water, bags for severed heads.

A reader listening for irony might find it in the very fact of that super-bland language. Tench has given us language as a kind of one-way screen; the words reveal, but they also obscure. You search the words for a tone of voice, and begin to wonder, how hard did Tench really try to creep up on the Aboriginal people so he could use those hatchets and bags?

But Tench, like the governor, is not prepared to record in writing the reality of what was being proposed. Let's take a few minutes of real time and real place. Let's say the six Aboriginal men are finally dead. The flies are starting to get bad. Someone – one particular individual man – is picking up one of the hatchets. He has to line himself up and get up close, to get a good go at the neck. This is a hatchet, not an axe – he'd have to get down very close. Necks are tough things, all that bone and muscle – he has to hack away. How many times would he have to chop at that still-warm human body? Blood fountains out of the arteries, gets all over his hands, his boots, his legs, sprays up onto his face.

Then someone would have held the bag open while he picked up the head – by the hair would be most 'practicable', I suppose – and stuffed it in. After that someone would have had to carry the bags on the long walk home. How would you do that, exactly? Would you hold it in your hand by the drawstring, like a bag of shopping, swapping from hand to hand as your arm got tired? Or would you tie it onto your knapsack and feel it bumping against the backs of your legs all the way home?

Two accounts of this proposal have been left in the record. The careful, precise, neutral language of both versions draws us into accepting the unacceptable. This seemingly reliable language lulls us, in fact, into a kind of collusion. It all sounds perfectly reasonable, until you tear through the screen of words and see what's behind it.

Which is where fiction comes in. Thea Astley understood very well the human reality behind the bland words left in the official record. She could put the heads back onto the bodies – and she knew how to put the heart back in.

A Kindness Cup, she tells us in the acknowledgments, is based on historical events: 'The impetus for this novel came from an actual incident at The Leap, Queensland, in the second half of the nineteenth century, but this cautionary fable makes no claim to being a historical work. Liberties have been taken with places and time, and the author happily admits possible anachronisms.'

But who cares about possible anachronisms when you have a scene like this, in which a posse of white settlers is ambushing a group of Aboriginal people? This is the reality of the scene that Phillip and Tench wouldn't articulate for us:

> The light was dry and brilliant. Nothingness was scarred by crow-cry, distant and sad. Only rock, scrub and the long line of fox-faced men moving in towards a massacre. They were only ten yards apart now as the cone of the mountain narrowed and could hear one another's snorting breaths and the clink of boot on rock . . .
>
> 'Now!' Fred Buckmaster cried. And they broke into a run, whooping as they went towards a cleft in the boulders.
>
> The world narrowed to a horror of shots and shouts and screams as they burst in upon the score of blacks herded into the inner circle of rocks. They cringed against rocky shields. One old man made a break for the side of the rock circle, but

Benjy Wilson brought him down with a bullet neatly placed in the centre of his spine. He lay moaning and twitching.

The men went forward and in, shooting steadily and reloading and shooting until the ground was littered with grunting men and there was blood-splash bright upon the rocks . . . Words, at this point, failed. Freddie Buckmaster kept thinking, 'Oh, my God! What now, what do I do now?'

The blacks moved back before him till they made a pitiful knot against his advance. He could see this pitifulness and the wretchedness of their defence so that some gland in him was disturbed to the point of his wanting to cry with shame.

Gland! It's the wrong word, and it's absolutely, precisely, the right word. Its wrongness pulls us up short so we're forced to imagine what lies behind it. There's something a bit revolting about the word 'gland'. It makes us feel the moment not in our brains or even in our hearts, but in our guts.

That word 'gland' is pure Astley – bold, original, pushing away at the language to make it new, using words to take an axe to the crust of the habitual. That word is what catapults us as readers beyond debating notions of right and wrong, beyond judgment or justification, and into the greatest wisdom of all – empathy.

The anthropologist Stanner said that Australian culture was 'earless and tongueless' on the subject of black/white history. How do you give tongue and ears to those hard subjects, and all the other unattractive places of failure, doubt, littleness of spirit? Astley chose to use the voice of fiction.

When she started writing, the Aboriginal people didn't have the vote, weren't counted in the census, weren't ever referred to except on the odd tea towel. She wrote, with the ironic, oblique voice of fiction, into that great silence.

By the time she wrote her last book she had seen a colossal change take place. What had been an area of silence and deliberate forgetting had become a commonplace, the stuff of public controversy. In Sydney 250,000 people walked across the Harbour Bridge for 'Reconcilation'. Thea had by then won the Miles Franklin four times and was probably Australia's best-known woman writer. A large chunk of those 250,000 would have read her books, laughed at her goldfish mouths and plangent nothings, and taken in unawares – like vitamins in a good meal – what she was inviting us to experience. That unmistakable and inimitable Thea Astley's voice opened up the world in a new way. She said things no one was supposed to say, and made you laugh in a sort of startlement. Making you laugh made you think differently.

The voice of debate might stimulate the grey cells, and the dry voice of 'facts' might lull us into being comfortable, even relaxed. But it takes the voice of fiction to get the feet walking in a new direction.

HILARY McPHEE
The Hunger for Good Talk

Hilary delivered this speech at the opening dinner of the Byron Bay Writers Festival, 2002.

This is one of those events I probably should never have accepted. But Jill [Eddington] is very good at festivals and lines people up months ahead when I have most trouble saying 'no'. Looking around I see at least twenty people in the room I'd rather be listening to than me.

But I accepted because I wanted to come. Writers have been telling me for years that this is the best festival in the country. I assumed that this was because you lay around in the sun talking to each other and having shoulder rubs and aromatherapy, but looking at the program everyone seems about to be worked very hard.

I congratulate Jill Eddington because, unlike most other writers festivals where everyone is crabby and feels put upon before they begin, she's managed to make this one feel good to be part of.

It's probably got something to do with the Festival having evolved around ideas rather than book promotions and marketing, which is how most of the bigger festivals have been headed for some time. The commodification of writing and writers out there is almost complete.

This is a very Australian writers festival, meaning that not only are we gathering in what is an iconic Australian setting – sun and surf and trees and huts and Mungo MacCallum down the road – but there are few if any visitors from global literature regarding us in a rather puzzled fashion, and this at a time when it's no bad thing to be talking amongst ourselves.

Although there are some of you here with new books, I don't get the impression you are only here to flog them, as seems to have become the rationale behind some of the larger older festivals. Byron Bay has a way of bringing together a large number of people from all around the country, and asking them to think aloud about ideas and the discussion of issues crucial to this culture of ours.

We need all the opportunities for public and private exchanges we can get, it seems to me. Especially now.

The public spaces allotted to playing with ideas and the debating of issues have shrunk in recent years despite the huge success of the Deakin lectures last year in Melbourne. The queues around the Town Hall to hear Robert Manne and Marcia Langton and even a virtual Edward Said said something about the hunger for hearing good talk – and that was before September 11 and *Tampa* and SIEV-X.

The gulf between the 70 per cent we are told who support the government's tough line on refugees and its US alliance (on both sides of politics, and notably among the under-40s and recent arrivals) and those who don't is as wide as it was in the Vietnam era, it seems to me. And the huge task of bridging that gulf – of finding new ways to ensure we aren't only talking to ourselves – is not dissimilar either.

There are a number of people here this year who are already doing this – fiercely and cleverly challenging the way the place is shaping. Max Gillies and Guy Rundle have brought back tough-minded satire just in time, and Rai Gaita, Hannie Rayson and Arnold Zable and many other people here have been writing about the unravelling of civil society and the brutal self-interest that has enveloped the place. Morry Schwartz's *Quarterly Essays* (their lack of female voices apart) have been one of the more interesting publishing initiatives of the last year or so – and three out of the six writers commissioned so far are here, too.

But the range of journals and magazines that can respond fast to public debate and the need to get ideas across to readers is at an all-time low. Literary magazines can't bridge the gap – there is no urgency in a quarterly no matter how good – and the daily papers (the *Age* apart, which is right now allowing space for issues) have a vested interest in not doing so.

The advent of sites like crikey.com – essential reading for anyone wanting to catch the first overheated whiff of political trends and corporate scandal – interests me. Perhaps we'll get a version of it as a platform for a wider debate. The ABC website, which is expanding into doing its own commissioning as well as providing access to real-time programming, now rates better than Radio National and its demographic is very much younger.

There are some good signs in book publishing too. There is more interest in commissioned nonfiction publishing and the beginnings of a less breathless approach to discovering glittering new novels, which I find hopeful. A few publishers, certainly more than there were a few years ago, are now prepared to invest in writers who must spend years on research to produce the substantial books we need.

And the few university presses left seem to be at last waking up to the wealth of scholarship and intellectual property they have access to. They are starting to imagine ways they might edit and disseminate this more effectively to wider readerships than in the tiny print runs someone I know well once described as 'turning books back into trees'.

Meanwhile the creative writing courses are, most of them, producing writers of fiction and memoir in rather alarming numbers. Melbourne University has 600 students in first year creative writing, some of whom will go on to postgraduate novel writing. But there's not much emphasis in many of the courses on rigorous tough-minded argument, or on what I clumsily call creative nonfiction where real-life stories and ideas are played with in forms that might engage the reader.

Writing has rarely been as important as it is right now in this country.

Words are needed more than ever before, words that identify what is going on here, words that cut through the mockery of the political correctness labels and slough off the ideological straitjackets and mantras that people stopped listening to ages ago.

Unless we find new ways to take our convictions apart and put them back together again we have no hope of persuading those who have stopped listening – let alone shaming our leadership into other ways of doing things.

New writers from our multi-ethnic diaspora must be given the opportunity to emerge (which means being published) – writers who can speak directly to recent immigrants and address their concerns, writers who won't allow themselves to become ensnared in a mire of institutionalised sensitivities and terminology.

This was brought home to me recently when a column I'd written comparing our reception to the Vietnamese boat people in the late seventies with boat people now got a larger than usual email response – mostly from people like me who agreed with me, which was gratifying.

But I also got a few replies from recent arrivals from Nigeria and Uganda who graphically described the chaos they had left and their relief in encountering Australia's strong stable government. It was only Anglos like me, they said, who were criticising the government, devaluing 'your country and your heritage' and not being 'proud of your British institutions'.

I needed to be reminded of the complexities and layers of response out there – as well as the clash of the cultures, which can be one of the best things about Australia.

We've always had a healthy suspicion in this country of any kind of alignment of literature and politics. The Australia Council for most of its lifetime has had to confront and try to answer accusations that it was knowingly or otherwise setting agendas, shaping art and writing. The scrutiny is essential and the question won't go away – and nor should it. It needs a book.

But probably few of our poets would agree with Czech poet Milosz who posed the fundamental question: 'What is poetry that does not serve peoples?' And we have not produced much in the way of political fiction in this country since the social realists, although writing for the theatre has been much more often engaged directly with issues around social unrest and dislocation.

We need words that ask questions in ways that resonate and slowly sink in. Just as a few American writers after September 11 asked the question 'Why are we so hated?', we need to find words to reframe a whole lot of certainties most of us took for granted were embedded in the place – but are now unravelling. Only writers can do it – find words that make waves or those that cause almost invisible ripples beneath the surface of the pond.

PETER GOLDSWORTHY
Travels with My Inner Toad

Peter first attended the Byron Bay Writers Festival in 1998 and returned in 2005 and 2006.

If you swallow a toad each morning, the eighteenth-century French writer Nicolas de Chamfort suggested, nothing more disgusting can happen all day. The first thing I do each morning (after taking the dog outside and watering a tree with it) is log on to the Internet, which offers toads a-plenty, freshly squeezed each day. I make coffee while the modem sings its strange high-speed whale music ('emforster' is my password: 'Only connect', a slightly twee in-joke that I have here outed), then sit and surf. First, my various newspaper Bookmarks and Favourites. Toad for the day? It's always a closely fought battle between human stupidity and human cruelty. *Compo shock: 'How can money bring back our son?' bereaved parents ask. 'We expected twice as much.'* David Hicks still in prison without trial or charge after three years. Isn't that the kind of thing we're fighting *not* to do? Mealy-mouthed politicians cave in to religious totalitarians who refuse to allow publications of a few cartoons, on pain of death. Excuse me? Did Voltaire never live? A teacher goes to jail because she had sex with her fifteen-year-old student who still loves her, and will wait for her. Excuse me again? Sack her by all means, but *jail?* How to make sense of this twilight zone? No chance, perhaps, but I surf on, compulsively, as if I can fit the jigsaw bits together.

It's taken me some time to realise that the driving force behind my compulsion is anxiety – the anxiety, not quite conscious, that I might miss something, miss the vital clue. The numbing abundance of choice in most of our lives feeds that anxiety. Bookshops paralyse me with their options, and the bigger the Borders the greater the paralysis. Restaurant menus similarly – these days I prefer to be told what to eat. *The usual please, waiter! Uh, I don't think you've eaten here before, Sir. Then I'll have what she's having.* Once again the problem is less anticipating the right choice than dreading the wrong one.

At first I thought the Internet might offer a more efficient way of assuaging my newspaper anxiety. My reading habits had been changing in recent years, particularly during times of political crisis – which is to say, all times, according to the breathless media. I found myself scanning the morning papers rather than reading them, partly because they seemed increasingly depthless, but mostly because of the anxiety that I might miss something. *Any*thing. The number of different newspapers I flipped through each day had also increased, particularly since the Afghan war. I told myself I was being a model Enlightenment citizen, trying to assimilate opinions from all over the political spectrum. In fact, I was mostly feeding my omnivorous anxiety. The Net at least allowed the daily quota of places, dates and body-counts to be scanned more rapidly and more efficiently. A whole morning didn't necessarily vanish poring over Editorials and World News and Letters to the Editor and Op-ed Opinions.

A whole biblical plague of tiny digital toads could be ingested cleanly and efficiently. For analysis of the depths beneath this daily froth there were journals and (less and less it seemed) the weekend supplements. Even here, though, the Net offered a superior choice of essay-length analyses. From *spiked* to the *New York Review*, from *Arts and Letters Daily* to crikey.com – so much was accessible without leaving a chair. Too much? Of course. One day soon a personalised artificial intelligence search-engine will sift through the toads and offer me a daily digest, learning from my past search-habits what interests me (or – let's call an illness an illness – what obsesses me). For balance, I hope it will be programmed to surprise me from time to time, using a randomiser of the iPod Party Shuffle variety, so that I don't spend my entire reading life preaching to my own converted self, politically and temperamentally.

Meanwhile, instead of making life easier, the Net merely added fuel to the fire of my obsession. And each navigator upgrade, or faster modem, or new broadband connection, instead of saving me time through increased efficiencies only made my bad search-habits more attractive, especially when I tried to get beneath the froth of ephemera and into the wine-dark sea.

And here is the core of my current obsession: the deepest trenches of that sea. Welcome to the Dark Side, young Net-walker!

The Net is less a World Wide Web than a collective Id, I decided while writing a novel about obsession of a different kind. The World Wide Id, I christened it, hoping the phrase might enter circulation – but I have yet to hear someone use it in my hearing. What I was suggesting – without getting too Californian – was that the Net is to some extent a cyber-manifestation of our Collective Unconscious. All our deepest, darkest and most thrillingly secret impulses can be found there, allowed out on parole in relative safety. Carnival fun, certainly, *maskenfreiheit*, the freedom of movement behind masks. But also the freedom of movement *without* masks – and especially without clothes.

Porn drove the development of the Net, along with the military. Love and War? Sex War and War, perhaps. The great thirst for porn also drove the development of scanner technology and video technology – because that's where the venture capital was. Porn will probably drive the next generation of Virtual Reality games, and porn already seems to be driving the development of robots, if only as sexual Pleasure Units (the recent SBS documentary *Obscene Machines* made for utterly riveting viewing). Net-porn is a baroque testimony to human (still mostly male) sexual ingenuity and idiosyncrasy. What a precise thing is a human fetish, how very narrow-spectrum its sexual turn-ons. Licking a lover's muddy gym shoes is fine, with a consenting gym-shoe in private – but why *only* gym shoes, and why only mud?

Of course there are far uglier fish to be found in the deep trenches of the Net than the odd harmless fetish. I first came across 'amnetophilia' here – the obsessive need of some people to have one of their limbs amputated. The language used is the California-speak of gender-reassignment – 'I don't feel myself properly expressed as a human being with two legs, doctor'. These are often tragic stories: if the victims can't get the limb sawn off surgically, they will sometimes attempt the removal themselves, often with fatal consequences. Needless to say, methods of persuading doctors to perform the operation (such as freezing the offending limb in dry ice so that it has to be removed surgically) can also be found on (where else?) the Net.

These are tough toads to swallow. I found plenty of others a decade or so ago when researching my novel *Wish*, which is a kind of Romeo-and-Juliet story in which the lovers belong to different species instead of different families. (This was the novel of which a patrician Spanish reviewer remarked, 'a novel with such a theme could only have credence in a country of rabbits, sheep, and kangaroos'.) So am I claiming that I only surf such sites for legitimate research purposes? That I only download net-porn for the articles, as embarrassed readers of *Playboy* magazine once liked to claim? Well, yes, as far as I can consciously tell. And unconsciously? Well, I wouldn't know, would I, by definition. But I do know that it is often a relief when my cyber-bathysphere surfaces from the crushing pressure of these deep-sea explorations and I find myself bobbing about among the froth – the Shane-texts, the Corby-circus. *So what if I've had half a dozen DUI convictions – hasn't everyone?*

I am back, also, among the sports results and sports analyses. This is an addiction that I seem, after many years, to have finally conquered. *Collingwood heroes show Anzac Spirit.* Being a caricature of everything that is ephemeral and trivialising about the news, perhaps such sports stories might be used as part of a self-inoculation program against the more toxic stuff, like using cow-pox against the small-pox.

I've travelled some distance and many gigabytes since my first Net-search more than a decade back. I remember it clearly: the Klingon Language Institute, from which I learnt to utter a few guttural words of that artificial but coherent language, in a shower of spittle. ('You should get a little damp when you speak the Warrior's Tongue.') At times the Net itself might be speaking nothing but Klingon; its images and stories are like a shower of spittle that covers me each morning. *Deathrow Murderer Deemed Intelligent Enough To Be Executed. Bin Laden Could*

Be Alive or Dead, claims US General. 'I haven't committed a crime,' pleads disgraced CEO. 'What I did was fail to comply with the law.'

Spit happens? The underlying challenge being spat at me is loud and clear: 'Understand *this*!'

And here is my core obsession: the need to understand. I've attempted to inoculate myself against this also, or at least to exorcise it – the pattern-seeking demon – by parodying it in fictional characters. 'Knowledge is an opium,' one such character sings in my libretto for the opera *Batavia*, who is 'suffering the cruellest of Needs, the Lust to Know and Find'. The psychiatrist-narrator of *Three Dog Night* is addicted to knowledge of a more Trivial Pursuits kind – a central structural irony of the book being his arrival at a near-complete lack of understanding of his own motives, or his wife's.

A possible future cure might come with those personalised search-engines. If I program mine to select only news items older than, say, a month, and only download essays with a word-count of more than, say, three thousand words, I might break the habit. I will need such help certainly, since I am too anxious to discipline myself.

The alternative is to surrender to that anxiety. Anxiety, after all, has its uses. Like all emotions, it must have conferred an evolutionary advantage on our ancestors or it wouldn't have been granted space in their brains. I see anxiety as a kind of internal search-engine in itself, or perhaps the energising force that drives such a search-engine, powering it down every alley in the wet-brain maze, every fork in the choice-tree, until all possibilities have been exhausted.

Worry, in short, is a brute-search program, like the early computer-chess games. It gets the work done. If there is a solution, it offers the best chance of finding it.

I once hoped that if I ate enough toads I might grow tired

of them, but such is not the nature of obsession. Toads, it turns out, are an acquired taste, and the more you swallow the more you want. Or perhaps (a worrying thought that my anxious search-engine has just thrown up) you are what you eat, and this is about my own stupidity.

Californian thought for the day: has all this really been about getting in touch with my inner toad?

DOROTHY PORTER
Numbers

Dorothy was a guest of the inaugural Byron Bay Writers Festival in 1997 and a guest again in 1999, 2002 and 2006.

      I get magic
        (sometimes I get more
        than I bargain for)

      but I don't get
        numbers.

      Numbers do worse
        than humiliate
          or elude me

      they don't add up.

      I am no algebra tart
        ravished

by the meretricious music
  of the spheres.

My eyes and nose
  never streamed
    with incontinent ecstasy
      through geometry classes
  as my disastrous triangles
    collapsed in a cacophony
    around me.

Perhaps it's a failing
  to grasp
    or even want
the utterly perfect number
  burning through my retina
like the utterly perfect morning.

Instead I peer
  with nauseating vertigo
into the deep dark pitch
  of numbers
like an exhausted mammoth
  dangerously tottering
    on the edge
    of a bottomless mystery.

RUTH OSTROW
The Violin

Ruth read this story at the 'Love and Death' panel at the Byron Bay Writers Festival in 2003. Ruth has been a guest at every Festival since 2000.

It was many years ago. My father had just passed away. In the divvying up of his possessions, there were only a few bits and pieces I really wanted. Dad's violin was one of them.

Though he played it rarely in his later years, he cherished the thought of it. Often pulling it out, stroking it, fondling it. Tears would well in his eyes as the memories would flood back. Memories of his own father playing the beautifully crafted instrument. Of his childhood, sitting in front of a harsh European teacher as he struggled to produce the magical voice his father could tease out.

Our home was always full of the sound of violin concertos in those early years of my life, pouring out of the record player with such passion. And not just classical violin, but violin in all its eclectic forms: fast, slow, the Irish fiddle, the exotic sound of

Middle Eastern fiddle, central European, folksy or blue grass violin.

Eventually my father abandoned his violin, preferring the trendier guitar instead. Or maybe the pain of his grief was just too great. He had never recovered from the tragic loss of his father, who died too young.

And when my own dad died, too young, I flew down to bury him, and to take back with me the thing that most reminded me of him. Everyone else wanted to keep his guitar. But I wanted that sacred wooden thing, so vulnerable, so fragile and filled with emotion. I wanted to protect it, clinging to it on the plane and wrapping my body around the case.

But what do you do with a man's soul?

Once home, I put it lovingly in our storage room, opened the windows for ventilation and placed a large, smiling photo of my dad on top. I tended the case, dusting it regularly. The one thing I never did, could never do, was open that case and take the violin out. Though I promised my daughter I'd give her lessons, each time she approached the instrument I would make some excuse and walk away.

It was as if by opening the case I would open Pandora's box. I was afraid that all the pain and loss of missing him would swamp me like a tidal wave, and his grief would hit me too. Because I believe energy continues to exist in objects long after the owners have gone, reaching out, touching, engulfing.

I often thought about learning to play myself. But would retreat. For if opening the case would cause such sadness, then what of the crying from the instrument itself, hand-made in Russia for my great grandfather, carried through generations of Jewish persecution and pogroms, thrown out of one country to the next, displaced and homeless until finally reaching the safety of Australia?

Like my father I, too, fell in love with the violin. So it was an amazing gift to find myself recently at the annual Woodford Folk Festival in Queensland, which attracts many of the world's finest, coming to bathe us in fast and furious Celtic, Gaelic, klezmer, gypsy or electric/rock violin.

But on the last day, during one concert, when a group of the best violinists and fiddlers in the world had gathered on stage to perform wild fusion, the emotion in my heart became too great and I suddenly felt the tears rolling from my eyes.

'Dad . . . Dad . . .' I whispered to myself, heart-broken that he couldn't be there to witness the pleasure of it all. For do we ever recover from our losses?

I imagined the notes reaching him wherever he was, and I let them take me to his soul, and I told him how much I missed him.

'Come visit me some time, Dad,' I said to the ghost I hoped was there.

That night a very mysterious thing happened. We had arrived home after days of camping and I was utterly exhausted. While I was unpacking, a stranger came to our door. She said she'd been at Woodford and had decided to drop in to Byron Bay on her way back to Sydney, to visit the man we had house-sitting while we were away.

Standing in the kitchen, while I chopped vegetables for dinner, she told me that she was a fiddler and had been blown away by the incredible violinists at Woodford.

'I wish I had my violin here now. I would love to play!' she said.

'Hey, Ruth has a violin. I've seen it in the store room,' said my house-sitter enthusiastically.

'I'd love to see it,' she said.

'I'll go get it,' said my house-sitter. And before I had a

chance to stop him, the instrument was put on the table and opened by the stranger.

'Oh . . . it's very old. I love old instruments,' she said, lifting the violin and fondling it gently. 'I'll get my mandolin and we can tune it,' said my house-sitter, who plays in a local band.

I wanted to protest. Wanted to stop them. But she was already twanging in tune with his mandolin, and before I had even caught my breath the bow began grazing the strings and my dad's violin began singing to me.

'It's beautiful,' she sighed. My husband stood beside me, squeezing my hand as I fought back tears.

And suddenly they were off together, our house-guest playing frenetic mandolin and she in some altered state of fiddling. Notes soared wildly into the spaces between us as dinner simmered on the stove and magic simmered beneath the veil of day-to-day life.

The violin was singing in pure joy. There was none of the sadness of loss that I had feared. Rather, its voice rang with the delight of being found.

And I knew Dad was there. In the room. In the sounds, mystical and profound. In the beauty. In the love pouring out of that woman's heart. He had heard my prayer. It was too coincidental that the stranger had come.

She stopped playing and put the instrument lovingly in my arms. I let the bow run over the strings. I let go a few tears, because I too had found something I'd lost.

NICK EARLS
Men at Work

Nick recounted this story at a panel on 'Men at Work' at the Byron Bay Writers Festival, 1999. He was also a guest in 2004 and 2006.

When I told my mother I was moving out of home to share with friends, she taught me how to make gravy and a reliable but unspectacular white sauce. She told me I wasn't going to be looked after out there. That adult life wasn't what it used to be, that a man needed two different sauce colours (minimum) to make it in the modern world. She told me that my favoured cuisine option of mixing all my ingredients in a bowl with crushed Weetbix and frying them was something that mightn't be greatly appreciated outside the tolerant environment of the family home. Particularly the one that contained a small amount of bacon, and that I therefore insisted on calling carbonara sauce.

And she was right. My early culinary offerings did not win the respect of my peers. But that was only the beginning.

Things were actually far worse. They were multiskilled way beyond the kitchen. I had a lot to learn if I was to function like any kind of man.

Damien taught me how to fold a jacket for travelling, so that however scrunched it gets in the bag, it doesn't get creased. He showed me better ways of ironing the shoulders of shirts. He showed me the bits of walls you never hit nails into.

So slowly I broadened my repertoire and became a more useful person to live with. And that's good when you're sharing a house, for far more than altruistic reasons. It's good because the more unique skills you have, the more people end up owing you, and you end up cleaning the toilet a lot less often than you had to at first, when you had no skills other than those involving Weetbix and a frying pan.

Fortunately, I graduated in medicine, which made me the household drug-free-sample provider. My other special skill was that, through my parents, I could provide limited access to a beach house at Caloundra. But some skills are pretty subtle and I've never had them. Like keeping plants alive for semi-extended periods, or always knowing places where we could get in for nothing.

But Damien had the most subtle skill of all. Damien dealt with all the household framing needs, before they were even apparent to the rest of us. Damien was good with framing, and I never even knew that lining up framing was a skill until I saw him in action.

He had a framer out Ipswich way, the family framer, perhaps for generations, and I think he came from a family that believed that all important documents should be under glass. So if anyone in the household scored a degree and left it lying on their floor, Damien would get fidgety until they'd let him sort it out. And within a week, and for only twenty dollars, your degree would be framed (not for hanging but for posterity) and he'd give you half-a-dozen true-and-proper photocopies of it witnessed by a solicitor. In case you might ever need them.

I was never sure when I would, and no one's ever said they wanted one, but it's probably good to have them. That's what Damien said. And in such a casual, obvious way that you couldn't ask.

In fact, just checking more recently, what you actually got for the twenty-dollar deal was your degree framed, two true-and-proper photocopies witnessed by a solicitor and six unwitnessed photocopies. Which only makes things harder. I live in fear of the day someone might ask for a look at a copy of my degree, because I have no idea which kind of copy to give.

No one ever makes that clear to you. No one ever says, 'Wouldn't mind a look at a true-and-proper photocopy of your degree witnessed by a solicitor', but is it what they want? Would just a photocopy look like you'd faked it? Would the true-and-proper witnessed copy look like complete overkill? Would you look like an enormous dickhead, turning the thing over and going, 'I got a solicitor to sign this, you know'?

So in the end I had to move into a line of work where no one wanted a look at my medical degree any more.

But there are some skills that no one I've shared a house with ever had. Changing a washer and replacing a pane of glass, to name two. Burying a cat, to name a third.

We got on quite well with our next-door neighbours. Their eight-year-old daughter used to play with her friends in our yard. Her cat spent a lot of time at our place too, and she loved her cat. Which, of course, was a bit of a bugger, since he died under our house.

This, we thought, was probably Michelle's first experience of a death close to home, so we had to handle it sensitively.

Of course, we weren't so sensitive that we couldn't each pretend for several days that Inspector Gadget wasn't dead. That he was just sleeping, permanently on his right side, while flies jockeyed for position on his eyelids. For several days each of us in the house looked at him as though he was a problem belonging to one of the others. Said things like 'Go Gadget Go' the way we always did, even though Gadget just wasn't going any more.

I think it was Damien who said, on the Saturday, that we had to face up to our responsibilities, preferably before the oozing started. Damien hated oozing. So we walked round to number sixteen. We explained things quietly to Michelle's mother, and pretended we hadn't heard her daughter's plaintive calling the last few nights. And somehow the three of us decided that the best thing, since Inspector Gadget was by now not as she had known him, was for Damien and me to bury him in our yard.

Under the tree that our other housemate, Lisa, called the passionfruit tree, and that we let her call the passionfruit tree even though we were pretty sure passionfruit grew on vines.

Damien chose the site, suddenly pretending to another area of expertise. I wouldn't have known where to start. I guess I would have just buried him way up the back. How did Damien think he was an expert in pet burial? How do you know these things? He paced it out, a spot away from fences and possible pipes and the Hills Hoist and any other perceived encumbrances.

Under the passionfruit tree, he decided. And told me, 'It should be safe here.' What did he have in mind? Grave robbers? Bad guys, avenging themselves on Gadget now that his guard was down?

Of course, he picked shale. He picked the toughest bit

of ground I've ever struck with a garden implement, but once it was picked that was that. And we manoeuvred Inspector Gadget onto the shovel with a cricket stump and not much dignity, taking far longer than we should, since we both had to look the other way and he kept rolling off. And we carried him to the passionfruit tree, his tail jutting out, stiff as a wire brush, his limbs rigor-mortised into a lying-down posture that we now realised was far from small.

And we scraped away at the shale, the dead cat beside us, just a hint of odour about him. And the more we scraped, the more we realised that this was no small task, and the more each of us became aware of a dilemma. 'That tail's sticking out a lot, isn't it?' I remember saying to Damien, giving it a bit of a nudge with the corner of the shovel. And Damien said, 'Yeah, and he is dead.' And I turned Inspector Gadget over with the shovel, quite gently, and still the tail stuck straight out. 'So,' Damien said, 'it's not easy digging this hole. And it's going to be nearly twice as big, with that tail. On. We could be here for hours.'

'We could,' I remember telling him, 'if I didn't have a wedding to go to.' A wedding I hadn't wanted to go to. A wedding I'd lost two arguments about and had to go to, and had been putting out of my mind as much as possible for at least a month. A wedding I would suddenly be very decent about when I picked up my girlfriend of the time less than an hour later. And forty-five minutes early.

And I knew it'd be boring, and it was worse than I'd expected, but every moment of it was better than what was going on at home in the backyard, whatever that ultimately was.

And the next day, Damien, creaking awkwardly and smelling of liniment and injustice, took Lisa and me down there to show us his work. The tree branch he'd strapped the torch to so that he could dig well into the night, the besser block he'd placed over the top to stop dogs digging up Inspector Gadget. And he said that he could put the blade on the base of the tail, and his foot on the shovel, but he just couldn't push. So Inspector Gadget was buried intact, in a totally cat-shaped hole, with an annex for his tail jutting out from one end.

And we owed Damien for that, of course. Lisa and I looked at the hole, at the work he'd been abandoned to do, and I think we felt a little selfish. And I don't know if he ever cleaned the toilet again.

That was nearly ten years ago, and we've all moved on. Damien now lives in Tokyo. He's a vice-president of one of the world's biggest banks, a job he doesn't love almost exactly as much as he didn't love being an articled clerk. He has lived in several countries, but always moves on specifically just before he feels the need to get close to either a pet or a shovel. It was a tough night that night, and not easily forgotten.

Not much, it seems, is easily forgotten. When I was writing my novel *Bachelor Kisses*, I assigned to its central character – a man with a somewhat slender life-skill base – a few of my original crushed-Weetbix recipes, including the carbonara sauce. And it was Damien who called me from Geneva and said it had been years since he'd even thought about the smell of cereal burning in fat.

It's been years for me too, of course. I've got some kitchen credibility now. All of my Weetbix recipes are long-gone and I'm fine with that. But I'm still interested in people, men and women, who don't quite work, at least not the way we'd like them to. Who have things left to learn and mistakes they haven't yet made. Because, in the end, that's probably all of us, one way or another.

JEAN BEDFORD
The Woman on the Train

Jean has appeared at the Byron Bay Writers Festival in 1999, 2000, 2001, 2002 and 2006.

She's always on the late train – the one that leaves Central at 9.38 pm and gets us home at 11.07, if it's running on time, which it usually isn't. I sometimes catch it on Tuesday nights, sometimes on Wednesdays, depending on when I'm teaching, but I think she's always on that train. Every night. I overheard her once telling another woman that she preferred this shift.

She's large-boned, of Islander descent – Tongan perhaps – and she's not young. Around late-forties I'd reckon. In some ways she reminds me of my mother's friends of fifty years ago – neatly dressed, un-made-up: even her frizzy short hair suggests their middle-aged perms. But they didn't have her breadth of shoulder, or her flawless deep-dark-honey skin. Nor would they have worn trakka-dax and high-top sneakers.

We're not friends, just nodding familiars, but I think of her as my train buddy. We both sit at the rear of the train, me as close to the guard's van as possible. On the journey up to town I sit at the very front; on the journey home, right up the back. I don't know why – it's become my routine, an obsessive habit. She sits in the next rear carriage usually and I always look for her when I get on. If she's not there I'm unsettled for the whole journey until we get to our station and I see her getting out further down the train. I'm always met at the station, rain, hail or high water; she never is. We half-wait for her on the dimly lit journey to our house, and she half-acknowledges this. Sometimes she walks on the same side of the street as us, fifty or so metres behind, sometimes on the other, darker, side. We offered to share our umbrellas once, on a filthy night, but she smiled a shy smile and shook her head and pulled up the hood of her parka. She trudged on, head down; in front of us, that night.

I imagine her, as you do imagine other people on trains. My politically correct super-ego knows the problems of imagining another race, another culture – not to mention another class, now that I am educated out of my own – but my instinct for story is stronger. She has sons, I think; she looks like a woman with sons. I imagine three of them – big burly fellows, softly spoken around the house. They still live at home, naturally. I doubt if there's a husband any more; he's either died or left. Or been left behind. She's a Christian, of course, some sort of decent, fundamentalist, total-immersion-based denomination: Church of Christ, Baptist, Pentecostal – we've got them all here, and a few more, with very weird names. From her speech (I eavesdrop whenever I can on the train) she was either born here or educated by Australians, so her sons would have been baptised in our local ocean pool, the minister with his cassock tucked into his belt, his fisherman's wading boots over his pressed slacks. She and the other members of the church would have watched proudly, singing those sentimental, rousingly harmonious Protestant hymns as the children, all in white, high-stepped down the slimy ramp at the shallow end, the cold salt water rising slowly up their goose-pimpled legs.

She doesn't live in the housing estate – she'd walk the other way, down the cycle track, past the cricket practice nets and behind the Catholic school if she did. She's moved on from there – renting a house with a garden, I think, up past the garage and the small group of local shops. She would have been able to do this when her sons began to work and brought their wages home.

She grows vegetables and fruit. She has an ancestral dream of a garden: women in lap-laps, with scarlet hibiscus behind their ears, bending and tilling the rich alluvial soil. At Harvest Festival hers are the biggest, most golden pumpkins, the plumpest marrows, the sweetest corn. She mostly grows what you can eat, but she plants sunflowers, too, and some bright perennials so she always has flowers when it's her turn to decorate the church. There's a frangipani in a large pot by her door and coming home some nights its perfume stills her for long seconds before she opens the front door.

When she gets in, around eleven-thirty, there's usually a snack waiting for her, and cocoa already measured in the cup of milk ready for the microwave. The older boys prepare all this before they head off for the midnight shift at the steelworks. (I don't know if there's a midnight shift, but there could be.) Daniel is in his last year at school and they will have made sure he's in bed by ten. She has high hopes for Daniel: he's bright and she hopes he'll go to university. Be a lawyer, perhaps, or a doctor. In her secret heart she'd like him to be a minister, but he shows little sign of a vocation. The others are good boys, too, Jake and Lester. They're handsome, energetic and always courteous. They take up a lot of room in the small house, but they're careful. She thanks God for them all, every Sunday.

Lester is talking about moving in with his girlfriend. She's ambiguous about this. She likes the girl, Annette (a hairdresser), but she wishes they'd get married instead. She'd like to help organise the wedding. She'd like a huge feast, supplied from her garden. She'd like Annette to wear frangipani in her red hair and to give her many grandchildren. But she doesn't say anything to them. It's her dream, not theirs.

Every Sunday she invites people from church back to the house for lunch. It's a standing invitation to the whole congregation and everyone knows they'll get a feed at her place if they've nowhere else to go, no one else to succour them. She leaves the vast roast – lamb, beef or pork, sometimes several fat chickens – on low heat while she's at morning service, the vegetables already prepared and waiting to be baked or steamed or fried. Crisp golden potatoes, fragrant onions, beans or peas or zucchini – depending on what is fruiting in her garden, sweetcorn, sweet potato (three different varieties: white, red and golden orange), and for most of the year fresh lettuce, rocket and endives, capsicum and meaty red tomatoes in a tangy salad garnished with her own fresh herbs. If only a few come back to eat, the leftovers will make lunches for the boys all week.

On Sundays she dresses in bright clothes, not the tracksuit pants and windcheaters over T-shirts of her working week, when she has to stand for hours on end – I imagine at some sort of assembly line. Some of the younger Islander women in the parish have taken to wearing a combination of African-inspired robes and their homeland costumes, with lush purple, green and orange head wraps, dangly gold hoop earrings, but she feels she is too old for this. She wears red and yellow shirts over floral full skirts or pants. She leaves off her sneakers for flat black pumps, or sandals in the warmer months. She glows on Sundays, dispensing food and warmth. Her normally quiet voice rises to shrillness and she laughs a lot, showing her splendid white teeth, shyness forgotten in her own house.

At Evensong she sometimes sings a solo in a rich husky contralto. Her joy in life and her good fortune throb through her singing. Her eyes close and she sometimes sways slightly as she sings.

After church, she cooks enough meals for the boys to heat up during the working week – casseroles bursting with carrots and potatoes and curries, rich with coconut milk – and carefully labels the Tupperware containers before putting them in the freezer. She will have cleaned the house thoroughly on Saturday: made the beds and done the washing and ironing, polished all wooden and shiny surfaces, weeded the garden, harvested vegetables and fruit. Lester or Jake will have driven her to the local Woolies in the small hatchback they share and she will have done the weekly stocking-up.

On Monday, with the whole morning her own, Daniel at school and the other two still asleep, she will wander round her garden, peering closely at new plantings, willing them to flourish, nipping off a burnt or caterpillar-eaten bud here and there, snipping back the flowering stalks of basil. Perhaps she will sit for a while, with a cup of instant coffee, her mind blank, under the canopy of her neighbour's rampant pittosporum before she wakes her sons for their sandwich lunch, then showers and gets ready for the journey to Sydney.

On Tuesday nights I might see her. I hope I will – I always look for her. She is my beacon of normality: hard work and just deserts and never questioning the futility of it all.

MUNGO MacCALLUM
The Best Weekend of the Year

Mungo has been a guest at nine Byron Bay Writers Festivals.

A few years ago I was rather chuffed to receive an invitation to the Melbourne Writers Festival. I had been to the big city festivals before, at least in Sydney and Adelaide, but that was in the days when I was young and briefly famous. I had thought to live out my declining years in the provinces, making a ritual annual appearance at Byron, a festival of immense personality but not really up there with the metropolitan extravaganzas.

Now I was on the comeback trail: set for the big time. The international superstars I would meet, the scintillating tales I would have to tell to my envious neighbours as we assembled around our rustic tents for our own little event next August. Sure, and I'd also win Tattslotto and be presented with an Order of Australia by John Howard. Yeah.

The first sign that my optimism might be misplaced came when I read the fine print. Actually I wasn't invited to the Festival as such; what they wanted me to do was to be part of a panel on the Sunday morning and to chair a session on Sunday afternoon – without pay, naturally. However, they were prepared to fly me down from Coolangatta at sparrowfart on Sunday and bung me back on a plane on Sunday night. I would actually be at the Festival for only about six hours – not exactly what I was used to at Byron.

I rang the organisers and explained that my understanding of the term 'writers festival' was that it included the suggestion of a festival for writers, a gathering where wordsmiths of various kinds could get together and chat. To this end I would prefer to come down at least one day before and stay overnight.

The organisers snapped back that they couldn't see the value in that. They had deliberately put the program together in such a way as to shunt people in when they were needed and then out again as soon as possible – wham, bam, thank you ma'am. They supposed they couldn't actually prevent me from coming down earlier, but they were buggered if they were going to pay for it. In any case, most of the sessions were already sold out so I wouldn't be able to get into them anyway.

I replied that in that case I couldn't see much value in coming at all. They said my publisher had offered me up to them, and as far as they were concerned that was all that mattered. I suggested that they rename their operation a Publishers Festival if that was what it was really about and that no doubt my publisher could fill in for me. After a few more acrimonious exchanges they agreed to rebook my flights and put me up in a cheap hotel as long as I promised not to eat, drink or make phone calls at their expense.

On this cheerful note we parted. I should have been warned: this was not going to be my kind of gig. I should have pleaded a subsequent engagement. But still, I thought, it was the Melbourne Festival: it had prestige. I might as well soak up a bit.

When I actually arrived at the Festival, I thought I must be in the wrong place. The venue – it was called The Malthouse – looked a little like a down-market funeral parlour. The impression was reinforced by the crowd milling around the entrance; almost all women, with an average age of around seventy-five and uniformly doleful expressions, they were clearly mourning the loss of something – perhaps the Festival itself.

Inside things were even worse; a pokey and dimly lit foyer led to queues headed for a medium-sized theatre and two smaller rooms, where the bodies of the participants were presumably laid out. Lack of space meant the queues overlapped and intertwined, leading to querulous scenes between the seniors involved. One of the problems, as I later realised, was that the sessions began and ended at exactly the same time in all three rooms; this of course meant near riots around the miniscule coffee bar during the brief intervals between panels, before queuing for the next event.

To add to the confusion, it turned out that many sessions had indeed been booked out in advance; devoted queuers were pushed aside by those with pre-purchased tickets. Crowd rage was not uncommon: walking sticks banged angrily on Zimmer frames where there was not enough room to swing a crutch.

To be fair, we were warned by the organisation that renovations were taking place and that everything would be more salubrious next year, but this was not much comfort to those who had hoped for a leisurely exchange of ideas in relaxed surroundings. The ideas were there; the program was in fact quite stimulating, with many distinguished writers and thinkers taking part. But it was hard not to feel that even those members of the ageing audience lucky enough to gain admittance were too wrung out by the time they did so to appreciate the performances.

And of course, as soon as the speakers were finished, they were whisked away, back to the airport – no time for informal socialising, not that there would have been space for it anyway. They were probably grateful to escape; I must admit that I ended up going to lunch with some Melbourne friends rather than joining the bunfight in the hope of a literary epiphany.

But there was the odd insight, and one which I pondered as I made my way back to the Beach Resort for the Byron Bay Festival later in the year. I was on a panel with Don Watson, author, historian and satirist, who had written the astonishing *Confessions of a Bleeding Heart* about his time with Paul Keating, one of the handful of political books certain to become classics.

I can't remember what the proposed topic was, but Watson used the occasion to bemoan the lack of public discussion in Australia; one of the problems, he believed, was the lack of a decent forum. This was the real importance of writers festivals: they provided a public meeting place for people interested in criticism and reform to swap ideas and form more permanent networks. I agreed with enthusiasm, but as I looked around the Melbourne Writers Festival I could not help feeling that there in Bleak City the opportunity was being missed.

Compare and contrast, as Gough Whitlam frequently said, our own glorious celebration. Having the climate to hold it outdoors, even in mid-winter, helps, as does the sprawling but self-contained arena we now have, hopefully, forever. But the genius of the Byron Festival is simply that it knows exactly what it is about.

From the start it was made clear that the Festival was for writers and readers – and also, of course, film-makers and film-goers, lyricists and listeners, and anyone else who saw words and their use as a vital part of civilised existence. Publishers, booksellers, literary agents, publicists and other participants in the industry were welcome, but not if they tried to run the show. And the writers were to be treated as professionals, paid at Authors Guild rates for their participation and encouraged to hang around for as long as possible.

But it was never just about an in-group, literary crowd: Byron has always been more political than most places, and the Festival has always reflected this. It is contemporary and connected, and this is one of the reasons the crowds are so involved – and so diverse. For me, perhaps the most uplifting thing about the whole wonderful experience is to see the groups of schoolchildren – as many boys as girls – chatting excitedly about their plans for the day.

There is nothing funereal about our Festival: it's one great big all-inclusive party. Like a night at the opera, it can be moving, funny, inspiring and passionate; and, unlike a night at the opera, our Festival is almost always about something important. And by golly, it's fun. As I was able to say triumphantly to Don Watson when I shared a platform with him at Byron a couple of years after the Melbourne experience, this is the way a writers festival should be. He did not disagree.

This is not the place to hand out individual accolades, but it is worth mentioning our tireless founder Chris Hanley. Where else but Byron would a real estate agent start up a writers festival? He put together a quirky team which somehow nursed the idea through the hard times to its present unqualified success under the incomparable Jill Eddington.

I am proud to say I have been a regular over the last ten years, and intend to remain one until I am gently retired to my wheelchair – although as the Beach Resort has wheelchair access I might as well keep going even then. Why not? It's always the best weekend of the year.

SUSAN BRADLEY SMITH

*The Long Grass of Talent:
David Williamson in Interview*

Susan was a guest at the Byron Bay Writers Festival in 2004, 2005, 2006 and in 1999 when she interviewed David Williamson. David himself was a Festival guest in 1997, 1999 and 2003.

David Williamson is arguably Australia's leading playwright. 'Born in 1942, he graduated in Mechanical Engineering from Monash University, Melbourne. Williamson has an international profile, many of his plays have been filmed, and he is the most consistent box-office draw in Australian theatre. Williamson dissects the pretensions and dilemmas of the Australian middle classes with great wit, writing predominantly realistically. Williamson's early work was associated with the alternative Melbourne theatre scene; his powerful early play *The Removalists* (1971) premiered at La Mama, Carlton; *Don's Party* (1971) premiered at the Australian Performing Group's Pram Factory. Later Williamson plays feature characters who are wealthier and more successful careerists. Williamson is a master at generating controversy and regularly engages in high-profile disputes with his critics in the newspapers. His attack on academia, *Dead White Males* (1995), purports to contribute to the debate on political correctness.' I wrote this biographical note about Williamson for the *Oxford Companion to Theatre*. It is a despicable task, writing encyclopaedia entries, or for that matter reviews, or anything that insists on capturing a life in 800 words or less. It borders on the terrifying, if not presumptuous, to think it possible that a life can somehow be communicated in such a manner. I am grateful, however, that I do not have to fit Williamson's career into the same amount of words today, because since then there has been much more – plays, of course, even one with Madonna in the cast in London's West End – but also the evolving story of an Australian artistic 'demo-aristocracy', with Williamson's sons both involved in the entertainment industry, and him and his writer wife, Kristin Williamson, founders of the Noosa Long Weekend Festival.

Susan Bradley Smith: Before we address the big questions about theatre and cultural ambassadorship, can we start with your career at home?

David Williamson: Yes, it's getting on for thirty years.

SBS: Is that a shock to you?

DW: No, no, no. It isn't, because I always wanted to be writing, and developing. It was perhaps naïve of me to think I could keep on doing it for as many years as I have, because the natural life of playwrights doesn't tend to be all that long. I was egotistical enough to think I could go on writing things that would interest me and interest my audience. Luckily so far that's happened. It has been a great privilege to have had the opportunity to utilise our best directors and actors for that length of time on such a variety of plays. When I started out I didn't envisage it would be a short-term thing. I thought, Oh yeah, I'll be a playwright from here on in. I'm starting to realise now how lucky I've been.

SBS: You were being bold and young?

DW: Yeah. I thought, I'm a playwright, that's what I do. But I didn't realise how theatrical, intellectual, artistic fashion dictates who's in, who's out, and how quickly you can be wiped off the cultural map. All of those factors hadn't occurred to me as a bold and arrogant young playwright. It was a very realistic older journalist, Colin Brennan, who took me aside and said: 'Look, they're gonna get at you. Not now, you're not going now, it's going to be plenty good for a few more years. The only criterion for artistic success is that you survive. Surviving is the only final criterion. So don't worry what they say about you if you're still up there and you've still got people coming to your plays.'

SBS: It seems to be very close to your heart that you're accepted as a writer. Your public debates – your public fights, if you like – about it have been as revealing as your plays.

DW: I'm basically insecure. In a sense I always have been, and too sensitive to criticism, which is one of my big failings over the years. I should have just shut up some of the time and said nothing. There was a significant fashion change which happened in Australia in the eighties, and I was not part of that agenda. I thought it was unjust in a sense. In the decade before, we were allowed to think that part of what we were doing was searching for a unique Australian identity, that there was something about this country that was different, and that we were articulating that to an audience who hadn't had it articulated for them before. Then, in just ten years, national identity almost became a swearword. We weren't allowed to utter it anymore, because we had to accept ourselves as a multicultural society that had dozens of identities, every one of them perfectly valid. There was no overriding, patriarchal, heterosexist male identity – which I was accused of propagating in my plays – and that was no longer permitted.

SBS: But you never went out of fashion with your audiences.

DW: I keep writing plays that are actually more intellectually challenging than some of the critics would have it. I read theory for six months before I wrote *Dead White Males*.

SBS: And your critics know this?

DW: Yeah. So in a sense my career since 1981 has been fighting back against what I saw as the critical homogeneity of putting me down because I didn't fit the new agenda. While we were in the nation-building phase of cultural identity from the seventies to the eighties I was okay, even with most of the critics. But once they'd decided that the sort of identity I was portraying was white, middle class –

SBS: And masculinist?

DW: Yeah, masculinist – I was part of the patriarchy and all that. I felt a certain injustice about that, so in a sense used the plays to fight back against the new orthodoxy which rapidly took over our universities. The theory wave imported from France started happening in the late seventies and became well and truly entrenched in a frightening way – Australia adopts intellectual fashions faster and more ferociously than any country in the world! By the mid-eighties, the whole university scene in the Arts and much of the Social Sciences had become Foucault-dominated. Truth was a difficult concept to define; a lot of what was called truth was just the power position of a particular group in society, more often than not a white male-dominated group. I didn't dispute any of that. I was just irritated at the fact that I knew it wasn't the total picture . . .

SBS: You've studied Engineering and Psychology. How has this affected the way you construct a play? And do you think of yourself as a social engineer?

DW: No, I don't. I see myself as a satirist and an observer of the human universals and I suppose what I was getting around to was that the social constructionist view of the world ignores the fact that we do have a biological past, we do have deep instinctive drives.

SBS: We can't all be deconstructed?

DW: We can't be. There are certain needs and wants and drives that are absolutely universal to the whole of humankind's history. The fact that I can read the Icelandic sagas and see the emotional needs for status, for esteem, the emotions of fear, anger, hatred expressed for very much the same things that we express hatred for, gives lie to the totality of social constructionism. I mean, the same drive and emotional needs are expressed in different ways culturally.

SBS: Is this your point in putting Shakespeare in *Dead White Males*?

DW: Yeah, I'm saying that great writers did tap into universals, and sure, there's a patriarchal flavour to Shakespeare's plays. You know, I felt a lot of the baby-being-thrown-out-with-the-bathwater being done in those stringently ideological years. Sure, the canon needs revision, it certainly needs revision in the direction of including many more great female writers, but when I saw attempts to elevate Aphra Behn to the top rank of playwrights I thought there was something phoney in this enterprise, sort of like an overcompensation.

SBS: The Australia you have depicted for us has grown from an arrogant, loveable Australia in the seventies to an anxious one in the eighties.

DW: Yes, oh yes. Cultural anxiety? Absolutely. I mean, the old A. A. Phillips cultural cringe hasn't disappeared from Australia, it was always a reality. And part of the bravado of the seventies was saying we're just as good as anyone in the world and all that sort of thing. But the reality has sunk in that we're a small country; nobody takes much notice of us. Even if we were doing good work it probably wouldn't be noticed because larger cultures don't tend to find smaller cultures interesting. How many New Zealand works do we flock to see? When you go over to LA and get involved in scriptwriting, the ethnocentrism is frightening.

SBS: Were you exotic as an Australian?

DW: I was seen as a competent writer who had written these screenplays with Americans in mind, but I remember the producers being terrified. I was not even allowed to go into a script conference and say *leftenant*. It had to be *lootenant*, otherwise they would have become instantly suspicious that I couldn't handle American stories, and stuff like that. We grew up with a second language in our head, and that language is the American idiom, so I could easily switch on and write convincing American dialogue in the screenplays, because we all become bilingual in that way.

SBS: Is that a less satisfying process?

DW: Oh yeah, yeah. I was assigned to the sort of films that were never going to be made in any case. So it was healthy for my bank balance but creatively bankrupt, and I drew out of that after some years of frustration, and decided that what I really am is an Australian writer. If there is a universality, for me it has to come through writing about stuff here. Writers in Australia are almost certainly doomed not to take a place on the world stage. We kid ourselves that the world takes a lot of notice of us artistically. If Elizabeth Jolley gets a big review in the *New York Review of Books* we think we're somehow validated, but the fact is, as my friend Peter Carey tells me, the actual market penetration of even the best of our work has been minimal. The sales of his stuff in America aren't huge – he still sells far more copies at home.

SBS: Talking to [award-winning London-based Australian theatre director] Michael Blakemore about his experiences of staging your plays in the States, he firmly believes that it was the newspaper strike in New York that stopped your run of *The Club* there being successful, because the *New York Times* came out with a brilliant review after the play had closed.

DW: Michael did a lovely production. Certainly the American audiences were responding in much the same way as Australian audiences, and it was still set in Australia. However, you could sense that they had a bit of a problem with the play. Our star recruit in *The Club* had just been bought for the record sum of $80,000, and the day the play opened some bastard American football star had been traded for eight million or something. I like to think Michael was right, that we would have had a hit.

SBS: I saw *Emerald City* at the Sydney Theatre Company, then reviewed the 1988 Shaftesbury Avenue production in London, and since then have met a few people who were also there and have shared memories of being an Australian in a largely British audience. The experience was like watching a foreign film, not being able to understand the language, with native speakers laughing a few beats ahead before you read the subtitles. You could hear the Australians in the audience laughing, and then the Brits getting it a bit later. Do you have any comments about the power of satire being an almost indigenous thing? Is it too deeply rooted in our culture to be successfully transported?

DW: I think that's possibly true. At the Shaftesbury Avenue opening night I didn't sense the immediate connection that happened in Australia for the same production. But when *The Club* was done at Hampstead, it was a big hit. I think that it was because *The Club* gave a more traditional picture of Australia that English audiences were used to – knockabout guys going over the top about sport. But *Emerald City* was positing that there was an urbane and reasonably sophisticated Australia. One of the English critics said: 'I could not believe my ears when I heard Miss Nevin refer to Sydney as sophisticated, until I realised that she'd probably never been outside of Australia.' The possibility of any intelligent life existing in Australia just wasn't accepted. I was out of step then with the tone of English theatre, which was incredibly rarified. Our stuff was raw by comparison. It was talking about direct emotions directly expressed, and it wasn't stuffing three layers into the subtext. It was of a culture that expressed its angers far more openly than the British culture. The pattern of behaviour we were capturing as Australian playwrights on stage was truthful to our culture, but thought to be gauche by an English audience that's learnt to define civilised behaviour as the absence of surface emotion and is skilled in deciphering what the emotional valences are in deep subtext. What I was seeing there I found deeply unsatisfying because it was a coding operation. On the other hand, when Australians are angry, they're angry.

SBS: Everything ends in a blue?

DW: Yes, and we say things we shouldn't. The English have refined contempt signals to high levels. Our world is a far more direct, confrontational and bruising world, probably far more like Elizabethan England. In Elizabethan plays they love a fight.

SBS: Have there been any problems with idiom when your plays have been translated?

DW: Paradoxically my plays have worked a lot better in Poland than they ever have in England. I've had a huge history at a high level in Poland, and all the plays have worked. So in a sense it's been easier. I think what happens, when a play goes to England, is that it brings with it the baggage of colonial dolts. In translation we don't have that automatic cultural sneer that the English still tend to apply to us.

SBS: You've written about some of the key points that have really mapped a shifting consciousness in Australia. Have you thought much about what's going to be happening in Australia in the twenty-first century? Do you plan your writing along with your philosophical projections?

DW: No, I just get fired up. I make the projection that if I'm really interested in something there'll be certain people out there in the audience that'll be really interested in it too. My plays tend to tap into ideological faultlines at the particular moment, when there's an ideological dispute I find very interesting dramatically.

SBS: How did you realise that you were an Australian writer?

DW: I realised in two ways. When I went to London and saw the sorts of plays that were succeeding in the West End, I (a) felt I probably couldn't imitate them and (b) didn't want to. On the other hand, when I went to LA, I realised that the only way to write for the Americans was to write about America, because that was all they were interested in. So, yeah, I did feel a kind of anger for my little tribe back here, because we have certain experiences I enjoy putting on stage. We interact in ways that I'm fairly sure I know something about. And it's all I can do.

SBS: I recall reading that there were too many literary functions going on in Sydney for you to enjoy your writing properly.

DW: A lot of demands can be made on you when you're known as a writer. A lot of people want a bit of the action and want you to do things. I'm something of a solitary type. I actually love reading, I really enjoy the pursuit. I'm quite happy now to be up in Queensland reading and thinking a lot of the time.

SBS: Do you feel that you have close peers?

DW: I feel that other dramatists in Australia are working in other areas of interest than I am to some extent. They're either writing from a gay ideological position, a feminist position, an

Aboriginal position, an ethnic position, and by and large that's the only form of writing that is found interesting by a lot of critics. So I do feel isolated, I do feel different.

SBS: You were talking about Chekhov this morning. Do you feel less alone when you consider international dramatic traditions?

DW: When I see or read Chekhov I feel that in some small way I am part of that observer tradition of watching human emotional pains, excesses and eccentricities from a slightly detached position. I'd like to think that there was a place for that sort of writing, because that's the sort of writing I do, rather than a writer who takes on board the grievances of a particular minority and tries to use it as a means of raising the consciousness of the rest of the population to the injustices of that group. That is a totally legitimate way of viewing your writing, but I'm more interested in stepping back and seeing the shadows of self-interest. I've been asked, often accusingly: why do you satirise people on the Left? The answer is, because it's not really appealing to satirise a Bjelke-Petersen. People like that are obviously out there for their own egocentric interest, they make no bones about it. It's much more interesting for me to satirise someone who says they're an idealist, but when you scratch the surface there's something other than idealism going on underneath. So, yeah, I do see myself in the tradition of playwrights who can stand off and be objective about the imperfections of us all, including my own. The greatest source of imperfections I've portrayed in my dramas has been my own. Maybe I'm deluding myself, but I do think my satire has been the hardest on Australian males than just about any other group.

SBS: Do you think it's time for some new critical work to be done about you?

DW: I'd hope so. I think that some of the stuff that's been said about me in the later years has been particularly shoddy.

SBS: Are we too incestuous in the Australian theatre industry? Is Australian theatre dead?

DW: The threat is more the aspirations of the new generation. They don't want to do theatre. To me it was terribly exciting to be a dramatist when I started. Pinter had just happened in England. Drama was seen by society to be an exciting venue for saying new things about your society. It's no longer the case. Now it's film. The best way we can keep the momentum going is by funding new companies doing new Australian work to a much greater degree, and try and get young writers interested in theatre.

In 2005 David Williamson announced his intention to 'exit gracefully and let all the young talent flood our stages'.

LARRY BUTTROSE
After Theory

Larry was a guest of the Byron Bay Writers Festival in 1998 and then every year since 2000.

Recently the debate about Theory and postmodernism has intensified, within both the academy and the media. For two decades widely accepted in university departments across the world, Theory increasingly finds itself under siege in academic journals, in newspapers and in the electronic media.

Theory, so called, is inextricably linked with postmodernism; in fact, in some quarters the terms are treated as virtually interchangeable. Theory originated from the works of mid-century writers and thinkers including Roland Barthes, Jean-Francois Lyotard, Jacques Derrida, Julia Kristeva and Michael Foucault, although its evolution can be traced back to the structuralism of Levi-Strauss, the linguistic work of de Saussure, and to Nietzsche's concerns about what language could truly express.

A central tenet is the denial of objective truth, positing

instead a never-ending horizon of subjectivities: that is, relativism, and deferral of meaning. Wrapped up in the postmodernist parcel is Barthes' famed 'death of the author', power relationships inherent in knowledge and language, the debunking of so-called Grand Narratives such as progress, history and artistic originality, and the shifting cultural–political implications of every phrase we might utter, every inch of newsprint and every frame of a film.

Living in Sydney during the 1980s and 1990s, I was inevitably aware of the Theory emanations coming from various university campuses, but whenever I came into contact with it I felt great relief that I would not have to concern myself with it, and kept writing. Some years later, however, after a couple of less than ideally judged life decisions left me sea-shortchanged, I was offered work teaching writing to university students, and quickly discovered that Theory would be a major component of the courses I would teach.

This meant a crash course reading the academic source works, which proved difficult as they are generally unsuited to reading. I say this because they fail to communicate their ideas in anything like a readily comprehensible way. Instead the reader is confronted with comically grotesque jargon, prose as knotted as terminally arthritic fingers, and syntax which would have me sending back an assignment to a student with a line drawn beside the offending paragraph and the suggestion 'Please Fix This Up'.

High on the reading list was Roland Barthes' *The Death of the Author*. His concern was the authority of the author over their work, which he saw as almost a tyranny of meaning, arguing instead that once a piece of writing leaves an author it becomes a mere 'text' with no inherent or inscribed meaning. Now, given the state of the world, one might have thought that authors rank rather lowly in the tyranny department compared with dictators, religious fanatics and arms dealers. Yes, the pen does have power, but one would have thought that, in the pecking order of wrongdoers, authors would be very much an afterthought.

But it is authors who drew Barthes' fire, because they dare to believe they have a profound, enduring and inextricable link with what they have created, their own work: that there is a unique and definite meaning, their own, inscribed within it. To Barthes, once it leaves the author it's just another scrap of text, a tissue of quotation amid a gale of them, and the only meaning is that which the reader gives: ergo, the reader writes the book.

His argument is of course predicated on relativism, that no two readings of the same piece of work will be exactly the same, and that these will be influenced by a vast array of historical and cultural factors. Up to a point that is true. But that is merely what we call difference of opinion, and it goes back further than Barthes, to the cave. Human beings have always varied in their opinions, because we have differing backgrounds, agendas, sense-perceptions. We've always known that. It is one thought that is definitely *not* original.

Barthes sledgehammers the walnut. Yes indeed, a variety of readers will reach differing views on a work, but to leap from there to the reader *writes* the book seems a wilfully ideological rather than logical leap, without proper justification or substance. But it was catchy, sensationalist, and it took off because it appeared to give us new licence to value our own opinion. But postmodernists didn't 'give' us that, of course: we've always had it. For the most part they've given us little more than a migraine.

Despite our differing opinions, society works consensually.

We may differ on almost everything as individuals, including how we sense, think and process information, but we still manage to work together, drive the roads together, enjoy friendships and relationships. This is because we achieve a working consensus. The same happens with literature, art, music and film. Despite widely differing views, a consensus is reached over time about the meaning, intention and ultimate value to us as individuals and as a society of a particular work.

Authorial intention remains a demonstrable factor in this consensus. How so? I broached this notion late last year in a lecture to my Theory-trained writing students, by asking that when they write something – and I had seen how they had all sweated and strained, crafted and cut and cried out in writerly anguish about how to get their thoughts down on the page – when *they* write, does it not come from them? Is it not integral to their experience, and when it leaves them will it not carry the meaning they gave it, the thing they intended it to say, inscribed within it? And if it is misinterpreted, would they not say: 'No, no, you misunderstood me. That is not what I meant at all. That is not it, at all.'

I suggested to them that I knew this to be the truth because that was what they, as authors, had said to me, their reader: 'You'll see what I mean when I express it more clearly.' They knew the ultimate meaning of their work resided with them, as it should. The same could be said for Barthes himself. When he had finished his piece on the death of the author and showed it to his first reader, if he had believed the reader was misinterpreting it, would he not have said: 'No, that's not what I meant. *Sacre bleu!* Read it again and you'll see what I mean. *S'il vous plait!*'

I made the further point in that lecture that there were some students delving into the life of Virginia Woolf, reading her letters and diaries, for indications of lesbian sexuality to cast more light on her works as part of the academy's ongoing 'queering' of Woolf. Why, I asked, would they be burrowing into Woolf's real life if *Mrs Dalloway* and *To the Lighthouse* and her other works were indeed mere 'texts', divorced from the life of the author who created them? Why the intense interest in her life if the text is all and authorial intention irrelevant? Why do we constantly delve into the lives of writers for that link between them and their work, seeking any deeper meanings to be gleaned from knowing more about a work's creator? It is because, human to human, we know that the individual they are is inscribed in every piece of writing they produce: that our work is an extension of our unique mosaic of experience, our very genetic code. In other words, the human search for deeper meaning goes on unabated, Theory or no Theory. Postmodernism may well celebrate the surface, embrace this Nokia world, but we as people know there is more, and go looking for it. Everyday inquiry gives lie to the myth of authorial mortality.

If *The Death of the Author* weakens, the corollary is a serious question for Theory itself. Is the relativism upon which it is founded itself flawed? If we do accept authorial intention, do we once more accept that there is a fundamental 'meaning' to a work, the author's (whether the reader chooses to adopt it or not)? How then can a work be regarded entirely relativistically? It would seem that it could not.

The more I looked at Theory, the curiouser and curiouser it got. For instance, for the adherents of Theory, all meaning is deferred, relative and subjective – except for Theory itself. Yet to work at all, to be intellectually acceptable, the relativism inherent in Theory must be an objective truth, a fact. That notion is either correct, or it's not. In which case, Theory becomes the only objective truth in the universe, like God, or a sun around which all lesser relative truths revolve like minion satellites. But if all things are indeed relative, as Theory posits, then Theory itself cannot be objective truth, according to its own tenets. Theory instead becomes merely the latest in its long line of so-called Grand Narratives. In seeking to debunk the Grand Narratives, it is one: indeed the grandest of all – philosophical dogma.

This is not to say that the questioning of those Grand Narratives has not been a positive thing in some regards, especially such notions as Progress (although this was already under heavy suspicion from other quarters anyway), but as Theory has ossified into orthodoxy, it has become what it once justly criticised. And what are we left with but philosophy, with all the doubts, flaws and untestability of philosophy, yet a philosophy that has been allowed to run riot through the arts, humanities and social sciences of universities around the world, creating a daunting orthodoxy and dominating the teaching agenda.

Intellectual and artistic movements tend to start with a bang, a feeling that *here it is, The Answer*, the delicious if illusory frisson of enlightenment, and for years there was nothing cooler and cosier to be part of than Theory. But such movements have their time too. They may run a decade or two, but generally run out of steam as the first generation of believers begins to question what got it interested in the first place. Theory has enjoyed quite a spell in the sun, but has been put on notice by the world itself, which has shoved its head through the filmy veil of Theory's relativities and said *actually I'm here, I'm real, and I'm hard.*

A number of commentators have written that the end came with the attacks of 11 September 2001. That Old Testament impact certainly did remind us that there is such a thing as the real, objective world, and there are verifiable, historical events. And while postmodernists may have been able to have characterised the first Gulf War as so televisual that its reality became intangible, it would be difficult to say that of the second one, where we have seen nightly images of people dead in their bombed homes, screaming children in hospitals, and systematised abuse in US-run prisons. We have seen the fear in the faces of the grunts of the US forces under fire. We have witnessed the invader's angst and confusion at foes who will not submit. This has not been cross-hair and blast, shock and awe. Rather, this time the Gulf War has been old war: horror, hate, loathing, self-disgust, the real things war has always been.

When Theory passes, one can't imagine it will be much mourned, even very clearly remembered, for that matter. Its impact outside the academy has not been great anyway. If you read book reviews in newspapers, you will note that words such as content, truth, worth, are still in use beyond the walls of the academy. Read these reviews and you will see little trace of Theory. This is because in the world outside the academy, it is by and large considered an annoying irrelevance. Books are received, reviewed, considered, appreciated, as they always have been, for their insights into human experience, depth, integrity, passion and emotional power. And it is consensus, filtered through widely differing opinions, and the passage of time, which creates what is a de facto global canon which includes authors of all creeds, races and sexual preferences. It's time the postmodern academy stopped kicking the tomb of F. R. Leavis, and recognised the reality of now.

Perhaps the greatest immediate problem of Theory now, however, is in its well-publicised spread from universities into the secondary sector, where it threatens again to turn 'English' into a taboo word. If the process of the past two decades continues in that regard, we will produce a generation which may well be able to discuss the semiotics of advertising but never possess the language skills to do it in writing.

The other problem is that, despite a perceived decline in Theory's hold in our universities, it may linger on simply because there is now a generation of academics who have been exposed to little but Theory. This is exactly the kind of problem which occurs when one kind of thinking gains too unchallenged a sway over others. When it falls, what do we have?

It is now three decades since Tom Wolfe warned of the primacy of art theory over works of art themselves, in *The Painted Word*. We have been through a long period where the critic has been considered more crucial to the work than its creator, where critical intention has been honoured but creative intention discounted. But as Theory's time comes, as now does seem to be the case, the implications for what we will teach, and how, will become ever more crucial. If we are to embrace neo-Classicism, where will we find the staff who can teach it, and how will we approach it? After Theory there will be a renewed search not only for meaning but also for how to teach it.

There is one other, perhaps even more crucial way in which Theory has affected our universities. The Left has been in deep crisis for some three decades now. The fall of the Soviet Union, the unabashed capitalist inroading of China and a chronic lack of self-confidence have left it virtually moribund. Some commentators even question whether the labels Left and Right apply any longer, and assume that everyone now accepts the inevitability of market capitalism triumphant in perpetuity.

Nowhere is the Left's crisis more clearly seen than in the Australian Labor Party. Despite the patent difficulties of the Coalition government, it has been inwardly focused, ideologically adrift: a party waiting for Godot. As such, though, Labor mirrors the general crisis of idealism in society, in which it has taken a panzer assault on working conditions to jolt the relaxed and comfortable into thinking about more than passing the Meadow Lea.

The crisis has been profound in the universities, formerly wellsprings of dissent. Beyond some protests mainly about issues directly affecting student life, the new generation of intellectuals has been rendered all but mute. Largely this is because, in these most economically 'rationalised' of times, undergraduate years are no longer seen as a time for free thought, rebellion, even fun. Now the years of study seem short, and those of potential unemployment long.

But is there another more surprising possible reason for campus conservatism? Postmodern Theory.

'What?' you ejaculate. Surely that's a preposterous notion. Isn't Theory almost always doctrinally of the Left – feminist, post-colonial, queered?

True. But while many of its notions may be left-liberal, with its enormous influence in tertiary institutions around the world Theory has become a smothering intellectual orthodoxy, a virtual reality box through which students are expected to interpret all. To understand Theory, students must first master the masonic code of the postmodern academy, as far from plain English as Madagascar lies from Siberia.

The academy has of course always had in-house languages, but Theory has taken this to a whole new level. The medium really is the message. Put aside for a moment *what* is being said, and look at *how* it is being said. Here in the guise of leftist politics lies a disdain for the democracy of direct communication. Here, in a textual assault on authority, is a seeming authoritarian orthodoxy, to be accepted no matter how incomprehensibly its dogma may be phrased. To demur is to misunderstand; to accept is to know, is to join the academic elect. As such, the dominant ideology of the intellectual Left for the past two decades could be seen as a kind of lefty-flavoured bourgeois elitism.

But worse, has it also weakened the progressive cause? As journalist Kurt Andersen wrote in *New York* magazine in October 2005: 'For several decades the philosophical ground has been softened up by the relativism and political correctness of the secular left, which succeeded in undermining the very idea of objective reality and of calling a spade a spade – so now in the resulting marsh, fantasies like Intelligent Design spread like weeds.'

In other words, the self-absorption of Theory has weakened the ability of the progressive forces to act. With its celebration of 'surface' and mockery of 'depth', the embrace of consumer happy consciousness and denial of history, it may have defused or at least confused the political will of a generation, especially those most exposed to it – arts and humanities students, historically the most radical.

The truth should be articulated clearly. The emperor has long been running naked through our campuses but everyone has been afraid to laugh. Theory is an intellectual playing arena, appropriate to the study of philosophy and linguistics, but its ideological colonisation of the humanities and social sciences, and especially the creative arts, has seen it dominate the undergraduate learning experience of a generation. It has dissipated the time of young people who aspired to find their own voice in literature, art and music, befuddled them with gobbledegook and drained their energy and creativity. And what is the relationship between creativity and Theory? They don't have one. They're not even estranged. They've never met.

One cannot of course prove Theory's contribution to student conservatism – the contention is as untestable as the tenets of Theory itself – but it does seem plausible. And while students have been confined to the academic barracks navel-gazing 'Am I real?' and 'What is reality anyway?', the Right has been steamrollering the real world with regressive, draconian measures and resource-driven military adventurism. While students have laboured over the omega code of Theory, where has campus opposition been to the Right?

After the announcement that he had been awarded the 2005 Nobel Prize for Literature, Harold Pinter stated: 'The job of literature is to engage with the world.' The same could be said for artists, thinkers and students – and indeed anyone of conscience. Or is that just another Grand Narrative?

ANITA HEISS

Aboriginal Writers on the Significance of Space, Sense of Place and Connection to Country

Anita was a guest of the Byron Bay Writers Festival in 1997 and 2003.

As an Aboriginal person I am often expected to be able to articulate my pre-defined, exotic and somehow tangible relationship with the land. This has become something I have written and spoken about as I attempt, as an artist and academic, to define myself in the world I have been born, socialised, educated and politicised into – my landscape, my place, my country.

I come from the Wiradjuri nation of western New South Wales. It is this country that I am patriotic to. I have, however, lived much of my life on Gadigal land, aka the city of Sydney. But my spirit belongs and will finally rest with those of my ancestors back in Wiradjuri *ngurumbang* (country).

Contrary to those I met when I moved to the Gold Coast some years ago, I did not automatically become a Queenslander. Even though I was born in Sydney I was never really a Sydneysider but a visitor, and I have never regarded myself as a New South Welshman (or Welsh-person, for the so inclined). My artistic creation has never strayed from being that of the voice of a Wiradjuri woman aware of where she will always belong.

Because I was born and bred in the city, I often write from an unexpected, yet very specific contemporary position, sometimes jokingly referred to as that of the 'concrete Koori'. My experiences and everyday life belong to a land whose sacred sites are now covered in tar and concrete.

However, when non-Indigenous people talk of 'stories of place' with an Indigenous context in mind, many immediately think of traditional stories, stories used by our old people to pass on cultural information and knowledge, or the history of a specific geographic region and the significant sites of such areas.

In contrast to such expectations imposed upon us, when contemporary Aboriginal authors talk of space, and consider our sense of place and our connections to country, we often do so in terms of the environments we live in in the twenty-first century, especially as many of us are urban dwellers and indeed the largest concentration of the Aboriginal population lives in greater Sydney.

That said, this does not mean we are not aware of our responsibilities for maintaining stories and knowledge of our traditional areas. It does not mean that we are ignorant of our clan groups or language groups, our roles as owners and managers of country and our moieties.

Rather, what it means is that we consider our connections to country through familial lines, as well as connection through long political, social and other cultural associations to particular places. Many of us also choose to write about the desecration of significant spaces in cities, which is demonstrated, for example, in the work of Samuel Wagan Watson who focuses on life in and around the city of Brisbane, in poems like 'Recipe for Metropolis Brisbane',[1] whose ingredients include:

> *1 utopian landscape with a blue river*
> *a mixture of European cultures seasoned with convicts*
> *200 years of conservative politics*
> *1 trillion tons of bitumen, steel, glass, concrete and treated timber*
> *garnish of exhaust*

Aboriginal literature focuses on stories of places that are too often forgotten, places like Cape Barren Island where history and heritage remain strong for the First People of that country. Our stories are of places that have been given to us once our own lands were taken, and how these created 'spaces' (for example missions and reserves) have become places of significant meaning for many, while often physically disconnecting them from their own country at the same time.

Aboriginal literature today is also the home of what I call 'big city dreaming stories'. These are the stories of those places that have developed around us thanks to the process of colonisation. Starting with the first point of invasion – Gadigal country, otherwise known as the City of Sydney and the home of Indigenous people from many different nations who have come to this place for politics, work, education and family.

The Gadigal (or Cadigal) land stretches from the south side of Port Jackson, extending from South Head to Long Cove (Darling Harbour). It is land covered in tar and concrete, skyscrapers and crawling traffic, international landmarks like the world's greatest harbour and Sydney Opera House and indeed Bennelong Point, named after Bennelong of the Wangal People. It was the meeting place for local clan groups that made up the Eora nation, who met for ceremonial and other business. This was also the site of the first recorded corroboree back in 1790. But the space itself is still alive with the heritage of the oldest surviving people in this world.

In 2001 Indigenous authors joined forces to pay tribute to Gadigal country and its ancestors and current caretakers. The resulting publication was an anthology, *Life in Gadigal Country*. Within its covers, designed by Khi-Lee Thorpe, Ruby Langford Ginibi writes of the curfew at Redfern, Brenda Palma writes about the story of the campaign to save Australian Hall, the site of the 1938 Aboriginal Day of Mourning Conference and Protest, while John Lennis writes about Cadi Jam Ora, a tribute by the Botanical Gardens to the Cadigal and their relationship with plants and the landscape of the area.

Life in Gadigal Country was published so that Australians, especially those living within the heart of Sydney, could better understand and recognise the ongoing living culture of Gadigal country. The history, the sites – both traditional and modern – the lives of people living, working and socialising there historically and today. Gadigal country remains a place of significance for Indigenous people from all over Australia.

Within the anthology, Brenda Palma's poem 'Sydney Real Estate For Sale'[2] comments on the changes to the landscape, and the difference in 'significance' between non-Indigenous and Indigenous Australians. She writes:

> ***Bennelong***
> Vogue
> Penthouse suite
> > World Address!
>
> *Corroboree below*

Kirribilli
High Rise
Harbour Views
    Prestige

    shell middens
    testify

Wooloomooloo
Townhouse
Walk to Work.

    The Gadigal yield
    sacred way

Bondi
Hot spot
Disco Life
One room
    To Go!

    Initiation
    ground

Waterloo
Towers
Going Up
    Inspect today!

    Wild eagle spirits
    Soaring

Maroubra
Lots
Prime virgin
Land
    A Steal!
    Ancestors wailing

Coogee
Classic
Studio
    Close
    Sporting Fields

    Bora rings
    circling round

Tamarama
Cliff-top views
A must
    Inspect!

    Shark Dreaming
    far below

Woollahra
Mansion
Heritage
    Location!

    Site contact
    Massacres

Interestingly, Palma writes about the wealthy suburbs of Sydney with Aboriginal names but few Aboriginal residents. And the only non-Aboriginal-named suburb, Waterloo, is largely made up of public housing and a very high Aboriginal population.

Within *Life in Gadigal Country*, artist and curator Brenda L. Croft writes about the permanent Cadigal tribute she was responsible for at Wuganmagulya (otherwise known as Farm Cove). Croft writes:

> Sydney is a place of many histories, some acknowledged, others hidden. The multi-layered Indigenous histories of Warrang (today, Sydney) are seldom heard. As an artist, the incredible beauty of this magnificent city constantly amazed me, with its location, and its historical links with the oldest surviving culture in the world. As an Indigenous woman, I long held a vision of bringing an acknowledgment of this region's original caretakers to the fore. Wuganmagulya, the original name for the site now known as Farm Cove in the Royal Botanic Gardens, is the result.
>
> Wuganmagulya (Farm Cove) is a sacred place, in the sense of sacred memories that are now being reclaimed. Appropriately, Wuganmagulya is on land that was reclaimed by the colonisers, for the area of the walkway was originally alluvial mud flats. The high tides still like to come up over the pathways at certain times, when the moon is full. A bit further up was once the site of Yulang Yirabadjang, a tooth evulsion/initiation ceremony for young boys, which had taken place for untold generations pre-1788. The last recorded ceremony was held in 1795, when hardly any people of the original clan were left, most having been wiped out by smallpox and murders. The Cadigal band, which occupied territory close to the first white settlement, were reduced from about fifty in 1788 to three in 1790.[3]

Travelling north from Sydney into Jaggera country, the city of Brisbane is dissected and written about by Samuel Wagan Watson, of Birri Gubba and Bundjalung heritage. In his most recent collection of poetry and prose, *Smoke Encrypted Whispers*, Watson uncovers and dissects the suburban landscape and the reader treks with him mentally and physically, searching for the perfect creative inspirational space for the writer. He finds it in Boundary Street, West End, in Brisbane and throughout its suburbs, and while doing so acknowledges the consequences of colonisation on his native tongue, in 'Jaded Olympic Moments':[4]

> *We're city people without a language*
> *And some of us have even less*

Watson also writes of 'Abandoned Factories' and drag racing, and in 'Deo Optimo Maximo'[5] describes the:

> *curvaceous segments of road*
> *like black smiles and frowns*
> *either gazing in the direction of the Pacific or the hinterlands,*
> *dark horses upon the clearing of the dreamtime tabernacles*

Aboriginal people in Australia live in a particular space; it is called the fringe – and it exists geographically, psychologically and socially, and it is from this very space that we often find our motivation to create.

If Tasmania is the fringe-dweller of Australia, then imagine what Cape Barren Island directly off Tasmania is, and indeed what that makes its Indigenous population. Part of the Furneaux group of Islands, Cape Barren became the first white settlement south of Sydney in the late eighteenth century. It was a seal-hunting colony where Aboriginal women were taken by convicts and sealers for their food-gathering skills and watercraft, as well as sex.

This, among other facts, makes Molly Mallett's *My Past – Their Future: Stories from Cape Barren Island* a significant story of country for Tasmanian Aboriginal people. This is not just a history book or the personal memoirs of a skilled storyteller known to most as Aunty Molly. Rather, it is a book that documents the living culture of the peoples from Cape Barren, like mutton-birding and shell-making. It is testament that history and heritage have been preserved, while identity has constantly been questioned, rights to land have been denied, and language for the most part has been completely lost.

The chapter 'Stories of My People' is a collection of photographs with brief biographies based on memories of the author and her connection to each person, and in turn their connection to the land of Cape Barren Island. She writes:

> There doesn't have to be any research done into our history today. Let us as Aboriginal Elders tell our own stories of the years we spent on the Island, coming away and mixing with the Tasmanian mainland, instead of others making up stories about us. It is time for our perspective, for our stories to be written in answer to all the past white interpretations.[6]

Travelling to Papunya in the Northern Territory, readers can consider the significance of space, sense of place and connection to country through the *Papunya School Book of Country and History*, written and illustrated by Anangu staff and students at the Papunya School in collaboration with children's author Nadia Wheatley and illustrator Ken Searle. The book was developed as part of the school's curriculum resources.

Like many of the glossy children's books coming out of houses like Magabala Books in recent years, *Papunya School Book of Country and History* (Allen & Unwin) is not just a book for kids. It crosses many genres, including history, biography, children's books and art.

With such a comprehensive approach, the book, I suspect, is a bible for the community that lies 200 kilometres west of Alice Springs, where the Anangu (the name of the local people of the central desert region) are the traditional owners of the land, and where English and Luritja are spoken at school, with the languages of many countries spoken at home.

In light of this it is easy to see that the audience is not simply the children of the school, but the community as a whole, and a broader Australian country that now has the ability to learn. Many would have gone through the Papunya Tula exhibition at the Art Gallery of New South Wales during the 2000 Sydney Olympic Games, but how many would have understood the history behind the peoples and country that produced those amazing works? This book provides that opportunity. The dot paintings of the region are internationally renowned, but how much is actually known about the people, the country, the history, the Tjukurrpa yard, the Dreaming stories of that very significant place?

Papunya School Book of Country and History, which is a compilation of drawings, paintings, time-line and information boxes, provides a comprehensive understanding of the history of Papunya since the first *Tjulkura* (white people) appeared in their *ngurra* (country) and the local people feared them as *mamu* (ghosts or devils). The reader travels visually through generations of stolen land, the killing of stock, Anangu resistance, the arrival of missionaries and the gospel, right through to the arrival of white explorers and 'devils in the sky' (aeroplanes). We learn about the first school in Papunya in 1960, and the 1992 High Court decision on Native Title, leading to the handing back of a sacred site of Pulka Karrinyarra (what whitefellas call Mt Wedge) in July 1999. These are all significant moments in the history of Papunya, and it is the simplicity of the book that makes such complex issues and events so accessible to all, especially non-Indigenous people, allowing those outside of Papunya to realise the local people's connection to that country.

Charlotte Phillips of the Papunya Curriculum Project says:

> For thousands of years, Indigenous people have lived in balance with the land. They see, hear and know about things. They know and hear with their eyes and ears. They read the country with their feet. They are turned into knowledge of the land. Their ancestors are their teachers. The country holds the stories in the rocks, rivers, hills and salt lakes.
>
> The Tjukurrpa (time of creation) is seen in the stars, sun, rainbows, storms and water. For thousands of years we taught our children about this knowledge. It is passed down through families. We learn by doing, copying, mimicking, watching, acting, telling stories, doing ceremonies, listening to stories from country and from inside our hearts.[7]

Travelling west, we head to One Arm Point and the story of the late Magdalene Williams in *This Is My Word*. Edited and illustrated by Pat Torres, the story is of the Nyulnyul people of the Kimberley raised in the confines of the Beagle Bay mission. She recounts the creation stories and special places of the area, her family history, the coming of the missionaries, and the resultant destruction of Law and culture. In writing of the 'Important Places'[8] of the area, Williams says:

Important place
For the Nyulnyul
People
For their food and
Water,
And these places were
Protected and respected,
Especially sacred sites
And the life supporting
Waterholes.
My family had special places
That were very important to them
And the places of great
Importance to my forefathers
Were Goorooloogoon
Or Murphy Creek,
And along the beaches . . .

There are many places in and around
The Beagle Bay area that have sites that are very important
to our history and culture.

The book is an attempt to not only document but share the dying language of the Nyulnyul people. The author says in her opening, 'I want to leave my stories and the list of language words and phrases behind for my family, so that they will benefit from my teachings and retain some aspects of the Nyulnyul identity.'[9] That Nyulnyul identity is connection to country.

Travelling south now and the book *Listen to the Old People: Aboriginal Oral Histories of the Pilbara Region of Western Australia* was born out of a Local Symbols of Reconciliation Project documenting the memories of local Elders. The aim of the project was to use oral histories of elderly Aboriginal people of the region to tell the Indigenous stories of Port Hedland and the Pilbara. These Elders spoke on a range of matters, including Understanding Country (the importance of land and sea), Improving Relationships between Indigenous and non-Indigenous Australians, Valuing Cultures (cultural identity and diversity), Sharing History, Addressing Disadvantage, Custody Levels, Destiny (self-determination and control) and a Formal Document of Reconciliation.

Visiting the Pilbara for the first time in 2001, I was able to obtain from this book the necessary information to acknowledge the traditional owners of the Port Hedland area, the Kariyarra People and their neighbouring language groups Ngarla, Nyamal and Yindjibarndi.

Readers learn about the history of Port Hedland as a gold-mining town and tin-prospecting and pearl-diving region. It was these early commercial activities that increased the contact between Indigenous and non-Indigenous people in the region.

The stories give an introduction to the area, including information about kinship laws, skin groups and local terminology. For example, the term 'whitefellas' has been incorporated into some Indigenous languages, and is sometimes pronounced *walpala*. The stories of this place matter for those of us who want to understand the foundations of the Pilbara communities that still exist and thrive there.

Travelling south-east we hear Jessie Lennon's story of place in *I'm the One that Know This Country*. Jessie's story is of Coober Pedy ('Kupa Piti' is an Anangu phrase for 'white man's hole in the ground') and the history of the area that spans Wilgena, Kingoonya, North Well, Ooldea, Tarcoola, Lake Phillipson, Finnis Springs and beyond.

Jessie Lennon is a natural storyteller from whom we learn about life of the Anangu, from their traditional eating patterns to their whitefella work with cattle. We learn how Lennon used to noodle (fossick) for opal as a kid, how camels were for a long time the only form of transportation, and where the name 'Coober Pedy' came from. The name was given to the area by Old George Turner. Lennon's story tells the reader about the area, from the 2,225-kilometre dingo fence across South Australia to the amount of water the Roxby Downs mine used daily.

As for mining, which is what we would expect to read about in a book on Coober Pedy, we learn about everything from hand-mining to the use of dynamite. The greatest explosion we read of, though, focuses on the British nuclear testing that saw Jessie Lennon and others get sick, and some die, in their sacred country. The author's vivid memories of bomb blasts at Emu and Maralinga are quite disturbing and place the reader at the point of explosion and fallout.

Like Lennon's first book, *And I Always Been Movin'*, which she self-published, her story has been told to and recorded by Michelle Maddigan and demonstrates Lennon's desire to allow the place she comes from to be seen by all. Readers can enjoy the vast outback through the eyes of somebody so cheerfully at one with the country she comes from, and see how it has changed.

In terms of those 'other' created spaces written by Aboriginal peoples in Australia, there's church-run missions and government-run reserves, and the institutions used as holding areas for Aborigines rounded up like cattle under policies of protection, creating fringe camps for fringe-dwellers, and removing people from what they define as home.

Reading Albert Holt's *Forcibly Removed* takes the reader

on a journey that is not sanitised or censored at all. The book looks at the inequities between Aboriginal and non-Aboriginal lives and the harsh realities of simply trying to survive once removed to the Cherbourg–Barambah Mission. A place where the white families had decent homes and the Murris were only allowed into town to work; where water would be carted from a tap a kilometre from their home; where the Murris were limited to fourth grade education; where freedom was restricted by a permit system; where segregation meant that toilet facilities were signposted with 'Not for the convenience of Natives'; where the one thing the Murris had in common was poverty. It's no wonder Holt writes of this place, that of the camps, as being 'dark and miserable'. But the fact that he does write about this place at all highlights the significance it has in the lives of many Aboriginal people today.

Likewise, *Aunty Rita* by Rita and Jackie Huggins considers life on Cherbourg Mission, where Rita was taken as a prisoner under the Aborigines Protection Act. She says, 'We had to stay in one place now, while the whiteman roam free.'[10]

The recently released award-winning novel *Home* by academic and lawyer Larissa Behrendt also talks about removal and the attempts of three generations of Aboriginal people to return home to country. In writing a review of *Home*, Indigenous author Terri Janke says:

> 'Home' for Aboriginal people can have two very different meanings. Each one evokes emotions. One meaning is the place where many Aboriginal kids grew up institutionalised, taken away from their Aboriginal families. The other meaning is the place of our identity, our heart. Home is the place where we originate; the place we yearn for; the place we belong.[11]

And there is 'No Place Like Home'[12] for Wiradjuri writer Kerry Reed-Gilbert, who writes in *Black Woman, Black Life*:

> *With all those miles,*
> *I've travelled*
> *There's just no place*
> *Like home.*
>
> *The bush it calls me back,*
> *Back to where I belong.*
> *To the land of the Wiradjuri*
> *Where they sing my tribal songs.*

Before ending this snapshot of the diverse ways in which Indigenous writers define what it means to have a significant space, a sense of place and a connection to country, I'd like to pay tribute to a sacred place that gives many writers from various Aboriginal nations inspiration. That place is Uluru, a shared site of spirituality and sacredness to all Aboriginal people in Australia, including Kerry Reed-Gilbert, who says in her 'Uluru Dreamin' 1'[13] from her collection *Talkin' About Country*:

> *Uluru Dreamin'*
> *Reaching out to me*
> *Uluru Dreamin'*
> *Connecting*
>   *– Belonging to me*
>   *– Becoming*
> *ME*

And award-winning poet Jennifer Martiniello, of Arrernte descent, also pays her respects in 'Uluru by Champagne':[14]

You
Are a flame in the blue
Dome of heaven
Eternal
Bubble of evanescent
Earth, the mother rising
In the spirits of her children
The land your
Magic
Spun
Between suns
Horizon to horizon
You are
Blue earth, red sky, deep shadow
The imprint
Of infinity on my soul

And so, you have travelled with Aboriginal writers across the land mass many here today call home. I hope it inspires you to read the words of those who have walked the walk, lived the experience of being Aboriginal in Australia, a country where we do not figure on the national identity radar. I hope you are motivated to use the writings of Indigenous peoples, as opposed to the copious amounts of non-Indigenous research done on us, to learn more about your own sense of place.

JOHN KINSELLA

Line Breaks and Back-Draft: Not a Defence of a Poem

John was a guest of the Byron Bay Writers Festival in 2004.

For me, the measure of a poem is the word, not the line. This is a re-lineation and slight editing (one line) of a poem published originally (1999) in John Tranter's web journal, *Jacket*:

And Everyone Gathered In Objection Yet Again
for Robert Adamson

And suddenly there was a presence,
as if it were worth something,
the pylons sticking up out of the water
like busted bones out of flesh.

A waterbird landed
but didn't make much of an impression –
a damp squib by comparison –
though a couple of fishermen

> couldn't take their eyes off it.
> Bloody voyeurs, somebody muttered,
> and the bird, as if taking offence,
> lifted and vanished
>
> into the confident glow of the poem,
> the crowd encrypting itself
> into the scene's diffident colouration,
> troughed and crested
>
> like the hum of the current.

As written above, it basically subscribes to the one-unit-of-thought-per-line, 'natural' if elided clusters of speech, and hypotactic clause structure. The lines, if not end-stopped, are weighted as points of sub-closure within the greater sentence structure of the poem. If the content is not conventional, the layout certainly is, with minor digressions. In terms of what's being 'said', the poem is expectedly periphrastic – it's a roundabout journey to get to the main point because there are many other possible points of departure in meaning and tone on the way. However, the predictable lineation limits the possibilities of this periphrasis, unless as readers we read against the line breaks – say, taking random points within an ensuing line as an end/beginning to the unit of (de-)lineation.

Within the figurative expectations of the poem, I performed this 'adjustment' in response to a discussion on the poem on a metrics chat site, recently brought to my attention. When I draft a poem with line breaks that go against expected or formulaic (in poetry) speech patterns, or, as the commentator on the chat site remarked, 'syntactical or rhetorical boundaries', it often begins in that staccato and stilted fashion of much lineated metrical verse. It's a set of ideas and images measured by line breaks – I gain a sense of balance and perspective in the draft, but rarely get the poem as I've seen it in my mind's eye. (I literally see poems written before I 'copy' them.)

In a sense, I back-draft. The original drafts are often comparatively closer to the linguistically controlled specimens that a more formalist poet or reader might desire. Sometimes I let them stay that way if it suits my broader purpose. But through a process of drafting de-lineation, often in fact relying on the physical measurement of a line in a particular font (which often changes when the poem is published) by way of 'weighting', using the centre of the line not so much as caesura but as pivot, I distract or displace the expected measurements.

Of course, for me, 'syntactical and rhetorical' boundaries are prisons. My poetry is a direct result of my politics and ethics, and form for me is a box to be pushed against; to be used pragmatically at times, but ultimately to be tested at every opportunity. I do not want my poems to give pleasure, I don't want them to be comfortable, and I don't want them to 'tell'. I want my poems to suggest and to bother – to irritate, and to instigate.

Language for me is a generator, and has an organicism that leads to the myriad creation of meaning (out of context); and so is form. Form is not simply the safe house of aesthetic and artistic control that allows us to know a text is a poem; form is not necessarily the guide to interpretation and instruction many hope for. It's how we are taught, maybe choose, to read that matters. I don't want to package a poem.

Even in the re-draft, the 'dangling' last line might somehow partially gain this effect – a resistance to the bracketings of the previous four-line stanzas – but equally it might provide a more restrictive packaging through suggesting total closure.

I see this draft as more anatomically correct than I find enticing. I don't want my poems to leisure or pleasure, but I do want them to allow for a polymorphously perverse interaction with both myself and the reader. They are fetishes, but hopefully with adjustable appendages. They will change with time and place.

The poem cited is not one of my personal favourites. It was written in response to Robert Adamson's great poem of collation and sublimated dialogue with voices of romantic and modernist urges in poetry, 'The Rumour'. It arose from the occasion of a boat ride on the Hawkesbury with Adamson, remembered a few years later in the context of re-reading 'The Rumour'. It's a poem about displacing displaced and re-represented voices. 'Packaging' it would be inappropriate. Here's what Adamson had to say about 'The Rumour' in an interview I conducted with him in the mid-1990s; what's crucial in terms of discussing the lineation of my response is that 'The Rumour' was always a poem about process, about a broader imaginary conversation on process and inspiration:

> **RA:** . . . And then I said that to Creeley, 'Ah, I understand, I understand,' and he was laughing. He said, 'Okay, okay, that's fine to understand it. I'm glad I can help. But now what you've got to do is write your poem in Australian.' I said, 'What are you talking about?' I had versions of poems, and that would have been early versions of 'The Rumour', especially that one I wrote before 'The Rumour'. Because it's a bit like Hart Crane, 'The Rumour'. I started it at the beginning and the end, and then filled in the middle. So one of the first things I wrote was that section called 'Everybody Gathered in Objection'. That was an early version. I showed it to Creeley and he said, 'Okay, what you've got to do now is write like Ted Berrigan, only you're

Australian so . . .' He looked at a lot of poetry in my house and he couldn't find anything that sounded Australian. I grabbed Bruce Dawe and Bruce Beaver and he said, 'Yeah, they're getting there, they're getting there as far as using the language.' He said, 'I hear this language. I've never known it before but I hear it in the air. I've heard it for three days and I can hear the tune you're all playing.'

That's the way he put it. He actually said to me to take the high art and put in the language of your everyday conversation. 'You're talking to me in poems that are much better than the poems you've got down here on the page.' It sounds so simple, it really does, but he taught me how to write down the rhythms of conversation and couple that with – this is just technical but it wasn't just technical – couple that with the language of high literature or high modernism, whatever you like, and play that off against it. So what will happen then in the technical exercises, you'll find – this is Creeley saying to me – you'll find that steeped in language like that, your subject will arise out of the language. You won't have to worry about where you're taking it, it'll come out; or, you know, it's just that when you find the right form you'll have the content. So you know, the thing about that was that, in a strange weird way, Berrigan came into that poem, although there are no traces of it in there.

JK: There's a rumour of it.

RA: Yeah.

JK: A fact, something we know, a scientific fact, for example, can be bent, can be altered to a certain end, can be propaganda-ised, if you like. A rumour inevitably will be, because it can't be reconstructed as fact. How does that notion fit in with the definitive poetics that you're trying to explore?

RA: In the book it's very important, that quote from Wallace Stevens at the beginning 'In the long run the truth does not matter'. Now that's really the first line of the poem. So I write, 'In the long run the truth does not matter', and then go on to investigate that. Because truth will be poetry and poetry is the one thing that cannot be corrupted.[1]

In my poem, the boat is flowing against the current, the swimlines are not those of the received speech patterns of 'old-timers' of the river Adamson has so vividly scored in his own poetry, and that I have heard around the river on visiting him. In some ways I feel it's harder to write against the line when lines are so clearly announced – that is, when they compile themselves in search of a chronological and event-linear format. I believe this is the case in the above version, with maybe the exception of 'as if taking offence', and there I have deleted the key 'on their behalf', going for a more conventional ambiguity through tight expression – a lie I've re-admitted to the poem, and maybe in tune with issues of honesty and untruth in 'The Rumour', but antithetical to the drive of the poem.

On the web chat site I have referred to, my poem was cited as unredeemable 'writing' (the title and first stanza – which remain the same across both versions – were not included, though a link to the *Jacket* URL containing the entire poem was), and its line breaks described as 'radical' and sometimes 'silly'. The protest was against a supposed 'modernist' urge towards creating lines of the same physical length, creating seemingly arbitrary line breaks which add nothing to meaning/sound etc. The general prosiness of contemporary poetry was deplored, and then the discussion sidetracked into contemporary poets being read solely by contemporary poets because of this. I have paraphrased this from memory, but think I have the basic gist of the arguments.

The idea that 'radical line breaks' (to quote one of my

critics) involve the breaking of units of common speech or expression and associative meaning might be allowed, I guess, in a kind of obvious declarative enjambment, where meaning carries over the line for a specific dramatic effect (and I'm all in favour of enjambment), or as an antidote to the repetitive staidness of the end-stopped line, in the same way that substitution of a foot in metrical verse brings relief to the reader, and good opportunities for the poet to show how elastic set form really is. This is all good, but working within the shape and framework of the de-formalised poem, one can, of course, go further. That's what interests me: keeping enough of the form for it to be recognised as coming out of some kind of 'tradition', but radicalising enough to question the heritage and the need for variation itself. It's self-damning as much as 'illuminating'.

If we view the basic reason for line breaks as rhythmic, and rhythm in poetry as directly connected with mood and meaning, then it inevitably brings us to the question of what necessitates a particular rhythm in the first place. Back in the Western Australian wheatbelt, and surrounded by paddocks, I make use of my brother's full drum kit to vent some of my . . . er, rhythmic urges. Drumming can drive itself. You start with a basic four-four beat – common time – then maybe slip into doubles, then compound a three-four beat into a six-eight, a waltz to Spanish variations, and build from there and break away (you can frame anything, do it in any denomination you want); or you can listen to (or hear in your head) a piece of music and drum to it with the same principle. My brother drums to words – lineated and non-lineated!

Either way, the ability to keep time is the skill; the art comes in breaking free of that – to my mind at least. And I'm not only talking about jazzlike innovation – divergences that ultimately take you back to a point of reference – but rather the notes of discord or arrhythmia that genuinely contradict the form you are working in or through. It might be that one aspect remains consistent – the accent of the drumming, for instance – a little like the length of the line becoming the measure of rhythm rather than the integrity of speech grouping or associative meaning. In other words, the line forces us to hear what we wouldn't hear by reading for literally expressed meaning (even where it's 'figurative') – it forces us to listen against expectation. It doesn't have to sound pleasing at first listening, but a different way of listening and thus hearing is suggested.

On the Microsoft Help and Support site on the web, the imperialism of correct expression finds its most paranoid and authentication-hungry expression. It's where the new media self-validate through the philanthropy of assistance and explication. It struck me: what of the line faltering between email packages – a common experience for poets and editors. 'Because I have problems with lineation, I have marked the end of each line with . . .' Anyway, here's a little MS internationalism at work:

OL2002: Posts Do Not Honor Line Breaks in Plain Text Format
View products that this article applies to.
Article ID: 287816
Last Review: June 27, 2001
Revision: 1.0
This article was previously published under Q287816

SYMPTOMS
When you create a new plain text formatted post that contains line breaks, the line breaks are removed when the Auto Remove Line Breaks feature is enabled unless there are two successive line breaks. However, the posts do not display any indication that this has occurred, other than the change in formatting.

> The information bar message about extra line breaks does not appear, either in the Preview pane or when you read the post. This processing appears to happen when the message is initially posted.[2]

Experiencing this lapse in day-to-day emailing might mean confusion of meaning for the reader untried in the vagaries of email, but generally we'd be able to nut our way through it. For the poem – especially one that doesn't use capitalisation to begin a line – it offers a real problem: a probable defeat of the original intention behind the poem? Or, even worse, a misreading that might lead to an accusation of shoddy craftsMANship. I WANT that software. I want my line breaks to falter and differ from recipient to recipient. One error in a book is just irritating, but a generative process that recreates text in an infinitely varied way is deeply appealing. It's probably as prescriptive as 'syntactical and rhetorical boundaries' – the same line-break 'errors' for all or most recipients. The third party infiltrates the text, but it's just their word against yours. The reader is left disappointed, maybe, but the error has been built into their expectations, their adjusted sense of rhythm. The irony is, though we can with a skilled ear detect line breaks when verse is written in metrical stanzaic forms, and quite often in free verse, it's an extremely visual way of listening. There's nothing wrong with that, but rather than sight and sound interacting it's more a demarcation of the two.

Gertrude Stein, in stanza LXI (Part V) of *Stanzas in Meditation* (Sun & Moon, Los Angeles, 1994, p. 201), wrote:

I wish once more to mention
That I like what I see.

We can hear that line break and don't really need to see the page. But knowing it's Gertrude Stein we might doubt it a little. Stein had an intense sense of the line (one non-believers called prosaic, despite its musicality), and where the expectation of a line break might be . . . broken. Seeing is to gain comfort. Milton's great sonnet of his blindness is a poem about seeing as much as loss of sight. Few poems embrace the blindness of the line, think outside the kind of drumming that simply keeps the beat. I've always admired Keith Richard's wise words about Charlie Watts, sublime drummer of the not-so-sublime Rolling Stones, that went along the lines of: 'a lot of drummers have the rock, but Charlie has the roll'. The roll happens alongside the rhythm, and is part of it, but it's also the slippage between the lines. Something to aspire to, maybe.

So, to cut a long story short, here's the published version of the poem with its much-drafted line breaks:

And Everyone Gathered In Objection Yet Again
    for Robert Adamson

And suddenly there was a presence,
as if it were worth something,
the pylons sticking up out of the water
like busted bones out of flesh.

A waterbird landed but didn't make
much of an impression – a damp squib
by comparison – though a couple
of fishermen couldn't take their

eyes off it. Bloody voyeurs
somebody muttered, and the bird,

> as if taking offence on their behalf,
> lifted and vanished into the confident
>
> glow of the poem, the crowd
> encrypting itself into the scene's
> diffident colouration, troughed
> and crested like the hum of the current.[3]

The poem itself occupies an indefensible position in terms of consistency in line breaks, but I stick by them and the means of getting to them – they were certainly more bothering to write than the first version shown above. I believe the poem gains in periphrasis, and though remaining fairly conventional in expression (it's not a paratactic poem, as such), the line breaks bring a suggestion of a dislocated clause structure. Readers are encouraged to read against expectation, to ironise their own process of reading through the poem ironising its own production. The observations have a sense of the matter-of-fact about them, even flatness (the 'prosaic'?), a participation in the rumour that displaces the process of witness, telling and insight. A possibly frustrating characteristic of the poem, for anyone reading and expecting a certain kind of lineation, is that the poem is primarily lyrical, though refuses to settle into the rises and fall of lyrical song rhythms. I would hope that the distraction and displacement of lyrical impetus makes the poem more volatile in its register, more evasive, and that, as Andrew Zawacki noted in his *ABR* and *Notre Dame Review* piece on *Zoo*, the poem 'plies an eerie natural and aesthetic transfiguration . . .'[4] In this case, the upsetting of the givens is as much a result of the 'radical and silly line breaks' as it is about the words used.

What's it about? Maybe it's just about an unidentified (choice or lack?) water-bird – the lack of naming encrypting the rumour of it having been seen. So, the biggest irony for me is that 'everyone gathered in objection yet again'. Maybe that's the other point of the poem. I'm sure Jo Shapcott felt the same when in the early years (late 1990s) of the *Poetryetc* email discussion list, a well-known British avant-gardist denigrated Shapcott's astonishingly technically accomplished poetry as being inadequate because her line breaks were supposedly 'without volition'. Coming from a self-proclaimed innovator, this struck me as being rather imperceptive, or even hypocritical. Women poets often get the line break and form argument thrown at them; I say, thank goodness that some resist expectations of form and convention. If Joanna Russ had been a poet rather than a science fiction writer, she might have had a chapter in *How to Suppress Women's Writing* (The Women's Press, London, 1983) on the male policing (or 'masculine' policing) of female line breaks. The gendered reading comes from the outside as much as from inside the poem-text. Lineation can easily become a security, a status quo, that needs on occasion to be resisted.

My partner, poet Tracy Ryan, wrote a response to the criticism of Jo Shapcott's line breaks as part of a series of poems entitled *bloc-notes*. I leave the last words to her:

Masterclass

You're nobody without prosody. Let me show you how it's done honey. I told the bitch, I said. I love her instinctive but without prosody, without volition. The definition of lack. I broke her line like a twig for her, like a waist so slender my hero hand could. Like a neck. Snap, a match like a rhyme. Tinder and flame, just begging for it. It wasn't force but you couldn't say consent. What she needs is a good enjambment. This thing is private. Lil ol me. The lines just lay down like that. Lil ol me. I have always relied on the kindness.

JOHN CARROLL

*Universal Rights – Singular Culture:
On the Clash of Civilisations*

John was a guest of the Byron Bay Writers Festival in 2004.

The London bombings of July 2005 served as a reminder that Western cities are now the target for a global Islamic death cult.

The most influential characterisation of what has happened since September 11 is that of Samuel Huntington, from a decade earlier. We have entered an age when the major conflicts are no longer between power blocks or ideologies, as in the Cold War, or even between nations. They are between civilisations.[1]

In this context, it is worth clarifying the ways in which civilisations – and cultures – are necessarily different. And the ways in which they are not. I want to argue against the Huntington view that a clash is inevitable. This does not, however, lend support to the 'universal brotherhood of mankind' perspective. That perspective assumes that all humans are the same. So, if only they would come to share common values and a common culture, then there would be no more conflict. Such a world is neither possible nor ideal.

At issue are fundamental questions about truth and belief. It is necessary to distinguish different types, or levels, of truth. There are three.

The base level is that of facts. Such as: Yesterday, I had lunch at one o'clock. It is true, but of no significance. The life of the individual is largely composed of everyday routines and habits that can be described in such a manner. But a life-story that is little more than a compendium of such banal facts is hardly worth living.

There is a middle order of truth – the ethical order. It is composed of the moral laws that constrain behaviour – the commandments or 'Thou shalt nots'. Many of these are petty, such as the rules of politeness, and these vary from one society to another.

The backbone of the ethical order is a body of cardinal laws. They are universal, that is, to be found in every human society. They include 'thou shalt not kill', 'thou shalt not strike or damage another human without due cause', 'thou shalt protect the innocent', 'thou shalt not betray trust', and 'thou shalt not lie about important things'. These laws constrain all humans, except those we classify as 'psychopaths' – people who transgress major interdicts without conscience.

Furthermore, all societies esteem courage, and scorn cowardice. A film clip of an adult jumping into a raging torrent to save a drowning child will be understood in all cultures, with admiration expressed for the courage of the adult.

There are also important laws governing other roles and conduct. There is the 'good mother', the 'good father', the 'responsible leader', and moral support for 'doing a job justice'. What varies from one society, or culture, to another is the specified circumstances under which it is permitted to break one of the cardinal laws. Some societies, for instance, have permitted infanticide – under the rationalisation that the baby is not yet human, so the normal prohibition on murder does not apply.

In the West, the recognition that all humans are equal in terms of the cardinal moral laws, and some of their derivatives, has come to be called 'universal human rights'. They apply irrespective of tribe, ethnicity, age, gender, status, wealth or power.

This is an exceptional historical development. Humans have generally been tribal. The tribal view constrains me to treat members of my own tribe, nation or culture justly, but those outside may be dealt with by looser standards. Outsiders – distinguished disparagingly as barbarians, gentiles, heathens, infidels, savages, and so forth – are legitimate prey to my self-interest.

It is only in the last half-century that a belief in universal human rights has become predominant in the West. This is one of Western civilisation's great achievements. It has its sources in the teachings of Jesus and in classical Greek philosophy, consolidated in the European Enlightenment, and, since then, developed into a staple of the liberal-democratic political form.

It may prove a precarious achievement. Further terrorist attacks on Western cities will test multicultural tolerances. France, with a large minority population of immigrant Muslims, is particularly vulnerable.

Technically speaking, our modern tolerances are not 'cultural'. They are moral. This takes me to the next stage of the argument.

The third and highest order of truth is metaphysical. This

is the order of capital 'T' truths. The central task of every culture is to provide convincing answers to the big questions about the human condition. They are questions of meaning – specifically, where do I come from, what should I do with my life, and what happens to me when I die?

The answers are provided through stories – what the Australian Aborigines call Dreaming stories. These are archetypal narratives from a long time ago, that provide structures of meaning, and ideal character types, through which each individual may make sense of his or her life. Each generation needs to retell these timeless stories in ways that speak to it.

Popular culture, from Hollywood to television soap-opera, taps into these stories. The classical themes are endlessly reworked – of the hero, romance, duty, fate, evil, tragedy and redemption.

Here, every culture is different. It is a core and incontrovertible difference. The archetypes of Western culture are particular and unique, coming from Homer and Greek tragedy, and from the four accounts of the life of Jesus.[2] They are very different, for example, from Aboriginal Dreaming stories. They are different from the foundation body of Hindu stories in the *Mahabharata*, although, in this case, there are some strong parallels.

Likewise, the sacred sites of culture vary – from Mecca to the River Ganges, from Rome to Mount Fuji. What they represent is not negotiable.

The great weakness in the West in the last century or so has been in the domain of its High Culture. The mainstream of literature, art, music and philosophy has largely abandoned its mission to retell the timeless stories in new ways, and interpret them. It has betrayed its responsibility to help people make sense of their lives and times. In its relativisms, surrealisms, deconstructionisms, postmodernisms it has denied that there are fundamental truths. It has often even denied that there are universal moral laws.

It is in the interest of everybody that all cultures are strong and independent. As the Aboriginal wisdom puts it, if you lose your Dreaming you die.

Insecurity about belief tends to breed a range of pathologies, including fanaticism. Indeed, the London suicide bombers were four young men living in the West, stranded between cultures, some of their families seeming to be integrating well. The four had reacted to cultural rootlessness by taking to a fundamentalist extreme. The September 11 terrorists looked on the outside like successful young American businessmen.

What about 'civilisation'? Samuel Huntington's conception is blurred. Western civilisation today stands on three legs. There is Helleno-Christian culture – the Western Dreaming. There is modern industrialised society – the product of the English Industrial Revolution and the ever-evolving capitalist economic system. And there is the political form of liberal democracy.

Radical Islam attacks all three legs. It is hostile to Western culture. This is partly out of difference, but mainly out of a perception of modern decadence. It observes loose morals, low standards of public decency, and a self-indulgent, profane consumerism. Osama bin Laden challenged: if all you in the West believe in is symbolised by the skyscraper, and a cosmopolitan city like New York, then I can bring your culture down. He added that soft living had made America cowardly; the moment its troops suffered casualties, they would be withdrawn. (In this case, the current Presidency has proved him wrong.)

Radical Islam is, secondly, envious of the power that has come with industrialisation. Bernard Lewis, the foremost Western scholar of Islam, argues that the Arab world has stagnated for half a millennium – economically, socially and culturally. It has watched on while the West has remorselessly gained in power, prosperity and influence.[3] Al Qaeda is driven by power envy.

On September 11 its targets were not religious or cultural sites, as one might have expected – the Vatican, Westminster Abbey or an American synagogue. They were the centres and symbols of Western financial, military and political power. It is as if they had been selected from a Marxist revolutionary handbook.

Al Qaeda is also driven by a lust for death and destruction. Osama bin Laden is unlike his predecessor, Ayatollah Khomeini, in showing no inclination to rebuild Muslim societies. His is a passion for destruction. In this there are, again, parallels with Western Marxism. Both share a paranoid delusion that if the enemy – in one case capitalism, in the other the West – is comprehensively destroyed, then miraculously the dreamt-of Promised Land will shoot forth from the ashes. Were Al Qaeda to paralyse the West, the truth is that, in the ensuing global depression, the Middle East would be the first region to plunge into anarchy and poverty.

Thirdly, radical Islam feels threatened by democracy. It is megalomaniac in ideology and practice. The worldview of Bin Laden is theocratic. Its ideal is pan-Islam, with all Muslim people and territories united under one head – that of the ancient Caliph resurrected in the twenty-first century. The Al Qaeda terrorist organisation is feudal in structure and Stalinist in its political ideals.[4] It is utterly indifferent to how many people it kills, and whether or not they are Muslim.

Theocratic Islam rejects the separation of church and state that has been crucial to Western development. The Egyptian Sayyid Qutb, the single most influential writer in the modern Islamist tradition, targeted the separation of the sacred and the secular as the worst feature of the West. The teachings of Qutb exerted a key intellectual influence over Bin Laden, and especially over his deputy, Ayman al Zawahiri.[5]

Without the separation of church and state, it is doubtful that Western science would have flourished, as it has since the Renaissance. The technological innovations that made possible the Industrial Revolution would also not have happened.

Similarly, the modern Western defence of universal human rights depends on the recognition that they are independent from culture in the big sense.[6] Culture is the preserve of churches – or at least it was, in the West, when the churches were still capable of retelling the archetypal stories.

Universal moral laws derive from a different source. They are constitutive of the human condition. They form a central component of being human, irrespective of tribe or culture. The state must endorse cardinal moral laws, whatever the views of any churches or other religious bodies.

The three legs of the tripod are inherently different from each other – that is, in their fundamental natures and their inner logics. Yet their historical evolution has involved complex interactions. Notably, the separation of church and state, indispensable to the rise of both modern democracy and capitalism, has its roots in the teachings of Jesus – a cultural factor. Even the monolithic Roman Catholic Church has largely respected this separation. Also, as Max Weber argued, the Protestant Ethic – a cultural factor – was an essential precondition to the English Industrial Revolution and thence the emergence of the capitalist economy. Inversely, the culture of theocratic Islam forms an impenetrable barrier to economic and political modernisation.

Osama bin Laden accuses the modern West of continuing the medieval Crusades. The accusation is false. The Christian

Crusaders rode under the flag of culture. In fact, so does Al Qaeda today. Human rights were held in contempt by the Crusaders, as they are now by Islamo-fascists.

The American banner heading the current Western incursion into Iraq proclaims 'freedom' and 'democracy'. George W. Bush has not the slightest interest in converting the Middle East to Christianity. His ideal is that of the Jeffersonian Enlightenment.

It will probably be a decade before a balanced judgment can be made about Iraq. I am not concerned here with whether the American neo-conservative assumption will prove correct, that the West needs only to take 'freedom' and 'democracy' to the oppressed and they will respond. Recent events in other Middle-Eastern countries, notably people taking to the streets in Lebanon, suggest the assumption may be right. But it is still early days. And idealism as a motive in politics is prone to triggering dangerous unforeseen consequences.

There is a case for the West exporting its civilisation, but only two of the three legs of the tripod. Above all, this applies to democracy and universal human rights. Whether there is justification for doing this by force is an entirely separate issue.

In relation to the second leg, the more a modernised economy spreads beyond the Western sphere, the less of a civilisation clash there is likely to be. Prosperity is a fairly sure antidote to conflict. And successful modernisation occurs principally through international trade, being less dependent on governments.

As for the third leg of the tripod, there is no case for exporting 'culture' in the high sense. On the contrary! Thankfully, the age of Western states backing missionary Christianity seems to be over, although there are churches, especially in the United States, which remain wedded to the evangelical mission of visiting pagan lands to convert souls.

In the wake of September 11, a serious internal multicultural challenge has risen for Western democracies. It has been further inflamed by the London bombings, in that the suicide bombers were not aliens, smuggled into the country, but second-generation British citizens. What should we tolerate, and not tolerate, within our own societies? Again, the tripod is a useful guide.

The economic leg supporting Western civilisation is not at issue here. In any case, the maelstrom of creation and destruction which is the modern capitalist economy obeys its own inscrutable logic. Further, most people who move to the West from other civilisations are drawn by the relative prosperity and comfort generated by industrialised economies. They are also attracted by the stability underpinned by liberal democracy. Indeed, it is the combination of democracy and capitalism that means that most things related to leading a materially fulfilling life in Western countries actually work. For anyone coming from the non-industrialised world, it matters that jobs get done, supermarkets are full, telecommunications function, and hygiene is good.

A democracy must apply its laws to everyone, irrespective of cultural orientation. This is uncontroversial. In addition, every citizen, in effect, takes an oath to an unwritten social contract. Citizenship brings with it responsibilities. These include respecting and obeying, as best as possible, the prevailing ethos of the society.

'Ethos' is hard to spell out clearly. We are usually forced to do so only when problems arise. As one Australian example: public opinion has been effective in reducing, even eliminating, ethnic brawling at soccer matches. It is 'unAustralian'. More topically, many Western democracies are being precipitated, by the London bombings and their aftermath, into a process of expanding laws against inciting violence. This may go so far as to ban public support for terrorism, and deport religious leaders and teachers who encourage violent acts against the West.

One aspect of being an immigrant is that you are a guest. There is an obligation to respect the laws of the house you enter. The hosts too are under the obligations of their laws of hospitality. In the case of both soccer hooliganism and preaching jihad from local mosques, the host society is right to impose its ethos.

What about the third, cultural leg of the tripod? There is no case for reducing religious tolerance. It is fundamental to liberal democracy, and the separation of church and state, that all citizens be free to set up churches as they wish, to worship how they choose. Our democracy guarantees enough social stability to allow freedom of culture. A problem would arise, however, and for any Western society, were a majority of its citizens – perhaps even a large minority – to become, say, Muslim. Even here, restricting religious affiliation would not be the answer. For one, it is impractical. Belief, in any deep sense, is not susceptible to prohibition or to force.

Such a 'civilisation problem', even emergency, could only develop because of weakness within – not threat from without. An inability to maintain the vitality of a culture's Dreaming has, in the West, fed the kind of rootless and compulsive consumerism that Osama bin Laden mocked.

But the reality is that the current crisis of meaning can only be countered by a return to the West's own cultural roots.[7]

It is the business of each culture, at home in its own backyard, to cultivate its singular understandings of mortal life. It is the business of all humans, wherever they dwell, to defend cardinal moral laws and universal human rights. Then, civilisations will be more likely to cohabit than clash.

PETER CORRIS
The Big Burn

Peter was a guest of the Byron Bay Writers Festival in 1999, 2000, 2001 and 2002, and established the Peter Corris Golf Day in 1999.

I sometimes feel a twinge of envy for Bob Ellis, Raymond Floyd and Dr Mike Donaldson. What could these men possibly have in common? Bob Ellis, as everyone knows, is the stormy petrel of Australian letters. Raymond Floyd is an American professional golfer, twice a winner of major tournaments and now raking in the cash on the USPGA Seniors tour. Mike Donaldson is a long-time friend from here in the Illawarra. He is a former head of the Tertiary Teachers Union and now back at his senior post in the Sociology Department at the University of Wollongong.

Well, Ellis and Donaldson are lefties, but Floyd, like most American golfers, shapes as a Bush voter. In their simplicity they thank God for allowing them to play well, as if the Divinity, if such existed, would give a shit. Donaldson played front row forward rugby as a youngster in New Zealand until he, in his own words, 'grew a brain' and stopped. Hard to imagine Bob Ellis as a sportsman.

The answer is that all three had their houses burn down, with the destruction of everything they possessed. Luckily, there was no loss of life.

In admitting that I feel a touch of envy, I don't mean to diminish the pain these men must have suffered, nor the economic loss, although Floyd was probably able to re-group the quickest, being no doubt insured to the hilt and able to hire the best lawyer in town. Still, those two major trophies . . . Ellis has written of irreplaceable losses of manuscripts, books, family memorabilia. Mike Donaldson rebuilt on the existing scenic site, but the loss of twenty-plus years of research and teaching and political activist material must have hurt.

And yet I still feel that twinge. This was brought on by searching through files and boxes for a particular document. I didn't find it, but I came upon sheaf after sheaf of forgotten photographs, tax documents, gummed-together folders containing manuscripts, and others, dating back decades, detailing the buying and selling of houses. Let's face it, as I fall into this mood I'm thinking of my workroom, detached from the house, burning down. Not the whole house – I have to keep this disturbing scenario under control.

The workroom has framed pictures and the odd 'honourable mention' certificate on the walls, along with tacked-up photos, maps and postcards. Nothing valuable. On top of the bookshelves are a couple of golf trophies – a runner-up, a monthly medal – from when I was playing an easy par 3 course. They are of a vulgarity impossible to describe. No loss. After thirty years of writing, the filing cabinet contains less of value than you might think. I went to Bob Ellis's house once and saw copies of bound produced and almost achieving production screenplays lying around. I flog my manuscripts off to the NSW State Archives to raise money to pay unexpected (and unjustified) tax bills. Not much of recent real value that I'd mind losing lies about. In my paranoia I copy everything onto a zip disk and secrete it elsewhere.

The discovered, somewhat musty, manuscripts I mentioned found their way over time into obscure spider-webbed holes. As attempts at screenplays – original and based on my novels and stories – they are redolent with disappointment. Burn, babies, burn.

The carpet – red-wine-stained and with cat hair embedded – is a gift from a friend; the TV and VCR are on their last legs; computers and printers are cheap. The movies taped on VCRs from the television over twenty years are available on hire for next to nothing on DVD. It comes down to the financial and family papers, photographs and the books. As for the financial stuff – tax bumf dating back to the year dot, conveyancing detritus, superannuation conditions and policy statements redundant because several times cashed in – good riddance.

Normally, the family documents would cause a pang – birth certificate for my paternal grandfather and obituary notices for him, employer references for my under-achieving father, my school and university records and those of my kids, plus birth, marriage and divorce certificates. Happily, one of my daughters is something of a genealogist and she's copied a good deal of this stuff. Much of it is replaceable anyway.

The photographs are a consideration. Grandparents, parents, siblings, friends and lovers alive and dead, children, a grandchild, people, places, parties. Photography being what it is, I know there are other copies of a lot of these pix, some in the house in albums in my wife's study and therefore safe from the hypothetical flames. When I look through the haphazard, poorly preserved collection, I see that the polaroids are mostly void of image and that a good many of the others depict places I can no longer remember. Some of the photos are sad – firm figures turned to fat, fresh faces now lined and sagging. They don't tug at my heart.

The books. A few date back to my early years: Idriess's *Outlaws of the Leopolds*, Golding's *The Bare Knuckle Breed* – birthday presents. The rest have accumulated over the past forty or so years. I've read them, for God's sake. Do I still need them? True, I use reference books for dates and facts and details, but all that is available on the web. Or mostly. The fiction, probably the most redundant of all (although I do re-read Chandler, Hemingway, Fitzgerald, McDonald Fraser etc. from time to time), is in the spare room and thus safe. The workroom books, apart from my own, are nonfiction— history, biography, sport, media. They have no intrinsic value; there are no first editions of note. These books are really just decorations, markers of the passage of time. Essentially ephemeral.

But what about my own books, about seventy of them? They sit on dusty shelves in no particular order behind the workroom door. I never even look at them, still less re-read them. The majority are paperbacks, deteriorating as the glue dries, the spines split and the ink fades. They are all in libraries somewhere and in better condition. There are collectors in the United States who do everything to preserve their collections short of bronzing them. My books strike me as something like sparks from the bonfires of my youth, shooting up and falling down, fun at the time. Extinguishable – a bad choice of words but you know what I mean. So let it all go. Be cleansed. See it as cathartic. Make a fresh start without all the triumphs, mistakes, weaknesses, cruelties, false hopes preserved in that amalgam of paper, metal and plastic.

Don't believe a word of it. I'm asking for a fire extinguisher for my sixty-fifth birthday.

DAVID LESER
Helen Garner and the Agony of Writing

David was a guest of the Byron Bay Writers Festival each year from 2000 to 2004, and again in 2006. Helen attended the inaugural Byron Bay Writers Festival in 1997 and also appeared in 2001 and 2004.

Where does a 55-year-old woman take herself when her marriage has collapsed and she is 'sick with sadness'? To whom or what might she turn when her family is far away and her friends in the grip of their own lives?

Well, in the case of Helen Garner, she'll go and sit in on a truly bizarre murder trial for a year, spend two further years agonising over whether to write anything about it, and then spend another two years wrestling with the beast before coming up with what is probably another bestseller.

Not that she planned it that way, or ever plans to repeat the performance. 'I could never go through this again,' she says now, rather wearily, from her Melbourne kitchen as she tosses mandarin peel into a bowl. 'I can't imagine ever writing a book like this again. I am frightened that people might approach me and want me to tell their story and I just couldn't. I couldn't do it again.'

Which is perfectly understandable given that in this instance a young man died slowly, horribly and in totally bewildering circumstances, leaving his family wild with grief. And yet Helen Garner, exquisite chronicler of people's lives that she is, was seized by this noble, almost primitive desire to bring Joe Cinque back to life, if not in reality then at least in print, where the decency of his character and the warmth of his soul might somehow seep through onto the page.

Helen Garner first heard about Joe Cinque in March 1999, seventeen months after the 26-year-old engineering graduate was found dead in a Canberra townhouse. A journalist friend had called to tell her about this strange case involving two female law students from the Australian National University who were charged with murdering one of the women's boyfriends. Details were sketchy. Apparently there'd been a 'special dinner party' at the couple's house before he was killed; something also about the young man's coffee being spiked with the powerful sedative Rohypnol before he was injected with heroin.

The women's names were Anu Singh and Madhavi Rao and, according to the journalist who tipped Helen off, Anu Singh was the one whose boyfriend had been killed. She also happened to be 'head-turningly beautiful'.

Helen found herself making tentative inquiries. She learnt that Joe Cinque had been killed on 26 October 1997, and that the two women, Singh and Rao, had gone on trial together the following year. A month into the proceedings, however, the trial had been aborted due to legal complexities and the women were now to be tried separately. Anu Singh's case was currently before the ACT Supreme Court. Helen Garner decided to sit in.

Anu Singh was the daughter of two Punjabi doctors who'd arrived in Australia in the 1970s when their daughter was still an infant. She'd grown up in Newcastle and after finishing school moved to Canberra to study law. A bright student with a photographic memory, she was also, like many of her friends, a 'keen recreational drug user'.

During 1997, Singh somehow reached the conclusion that she was suffering from a fatal muscle-wasting disease brought on by her consumption – in her 'endless quest for thinness' – of large doses of the vomit-inducing syrup ipecac. Although she'd been dieting since the age of eleven, she blamed this and certain other aspects of her life on her boyfriend of nearly two years, Joe Cinque.

Helen pored over the press-clippings and court transcripts of the case so far. They revealed that Singh had boasted to her friends about how well-versed she was in both psychiatry and the law and how easy it was to convince people that someone was insane. She often spoke of suicide and, to some friends, about how she would one day drug Joe so that he would be asleep when she killed herself, or, alternatively, that she would take him with her.

Anu Singh's best friend, Madhavi Rao, also an Australian of Indian descent, was said to have been privy to Singh's plans from the beginning. The two of them had purportedly researched suicide methods at the university library, and after a process of elimination had ended up taking heroin-injecting lessons from fellow law students. The students were apparently more than happy to buy the heroin for them in downtown Canberra and then show them the exact dosage required to cause immediate death.

On the weekend that Joe Cinque died, a number of people were invited to a dinner party at his and Singh's townhouse, but it was only after they went home that Singh laced Joe's coffee with Rohypnol. While he was unconscious she gave him a lethal hit of heroin. But instead of dying quickly and quietly – as she'd been advised he would – Joe hovered on the edge for hours, right through the night and into the following morning.

At around noon on Sunday, October 26, Singh, according to the press-cuttings, started to get cold feet. She phoned the friend who had procured the Rohypnol for her and told her what she'd done; how Joe's lips were now 'a tiny bit blue, and he was taking a breath every ten seconds or so'.

She begged the friend, a sometime heroin user herself, to come over and revive him. The friend refused. She told Singh to dial emergency at once. Singh went into hysterics. *What would Joe say if the paramedics revived him and he learnt what she'd done?* The friend stood firm. Singh dialled 000 but the ambulance arrived too late.

If this story sounds too unbelievably fantastic for words, then consider this. A number of Anu Singh and Madhavi Rao's friends had heard talk of what one described as a 'last night on earth party'. They'd just refused to believe it. Some of those friends are now lawyers.

Consider also that it took two attempts on Joe Cinque's life for him to die. That's because there were two 'farewell' dinner parties held for him during that fateful Canberra spring, not one.

The first one was held on the Monday night, the second on the following Friday night. There were suggestions that Singh might have laced Joe's coffee with Valium on the Monday night and then unsuccessfully tried to inject him with heroin while he was sleeping. (This attempt failed, apparently because Joe was restless and kept moving in his sleep.) The Crown, however, didn't have enough evidence to pursue this initial attempt on Joe's life and so, much to the outrage of the Cinque family, dropped the matter.

The Crown also couldn't prove that Joe had been injected the following Friday night after the second dinner party, only that he'd been injected with heroin on the Sunday and then choked to death on his own vomit.

(The evidence couldn't show with certainty whether he'd been injected twice on the Sunday, despite the fact that the morphine concentrations found in his body were consistent with him having been injected first at about 3 am on Sunday and then again at sometime between 10 and 11 that same morning.)

What appears to have happened is that he was slipped large quantities of Rohypnol around midnight on the Friday and then fell into a state of unconsciousness until Saturday evening. When he finally got up, he'd apparently staggered around the house throwing away all the drugs he could find, but he didn't bargain on being drugged again after dinner with another massive dose of Rohypnol. (The heroin was successfully injected later.)

Did this mean that he knew his girlfriend was trying to poison him? His parents think not.

'On Monday night,' Nino Cinque told Helen, 'when they had the first party, they give him just Valium tablets. When he was sleeping, he keep moving around – they can't reach him.'

'Can't get the vein,' says his wife. 'Joe wasn't stupid. After the party on the Monday, if he knew she was trying to kill him, he would have left straightaway.

'When we went to the house to get his stuff, the day after

he passed away, we couldn't find his set of suitcases, his overnight bag, the hanger for his suits . . . My son dress beautifully. He had at least twelve good shirts, Country Road. But we only found two shirts. I said this to the police straightaway, "Joe hasn't got his stuff. He was going to move out . . ."

'Look. This [diary] is from his work . . . His diary said he was gonna leave her. On Monday 27, here it is, look – *Two o'clock, get ready to move.* See? Then he's got an arrow down to six o'clock that night – *Move urgent today.*

'He must realise after the party on Monday 20 that there was something wrong. He was gonna move out. He was gonna move out, and she knew, and that's why she killed him.

'He didn't know nothing about the Friday party. If you had one on the Monday why you want to have another one the same week? So when he came home from work on the Friday, she had a party ready, and that's it. He never left.'

Anu Singh was a woman who, as Helen Garner freely admits, raised her 'girl-hackles'. She was to Helen the classic type – a sex bomb with a 'frantic need to be found attractive'. Singh had admitted giving Joe the lethal dose of heroin on the Sunday, but her lawyers successfully argued that she was a 'disturbed and suicidal young woman', a woman who'd become lost in the deluded belief that she was dying from a degenerative illness. Yes, she accepted the tragedy of what she'd done, but this was not a man she disliked. To the contrary, this was a man whom she planned to marry. This was a case, therefore, of diminished responsibility.

In April 1999 Anu Singh was found not guilty of murder but, rather, guilty of manslaughter. Two months later she was sentenced to ten years in prison, with a backdated four-year non-parole period. She was due for release on 26 October 2001, four years to the day since she'd killed Joe Cinque.

(During her time in prison, Singh completed her law degree as well as a masters degree in criminology. At the time of writing, she was back in prison after breaching her parole conditions.)

For her part, Madhavi Rao, a far less dynamic woman than Singh, a tennis player, a practitioner of yoga and meditation with a commitment to the environment, was charged by the Crown with having shared a common purpose to kill Joe. The court heard that Rao had told two puzzled colleagues that 'the worst thing in the Crimes Act' had been attempted at a dinner party on Monday, 20 October 1997, and that it would be tried again the following weekend.

Her lawyers argued there was no evidence of the Monday attempt and that no one could be sure that when Rao went into the bedroom and saw Joe Cinque lying comatose on the following Sunday morning that he'd already been given a fatal injection. Her failure to act was hardly a measure of culpability. Even though she was his friend and had heard Singh talking up what she might do to herself and/or Joe, this friendship in itself didn't create a duty of care. Duty of care was different from duty to act.

In December 1999 Madhavi Rao was acquitted. She has since married and left the country.

The Cinque family was shattered. 'Rot in hell, you bitch,' Joe's distraught mother, Maria, had yelled when Singh was led from the court. 'What's happening here?' she cried again when Rao was found not guilty. 'They kill my son.'

Helen Garner has always brandished a fist at convention. When she was a university student in the 1960s she slept with her tutor. When she was a teacher at Fitzroy High School in 1972 she was sacked for daring to discuss sex – in explicit terms – with her students. As a young journalist, she chose to write for alternative publications like the feminist newspaper *Vashti's Voice*, and the alternative newspaper *The Digger*. As a 1960s feminist, she worked for abortion law reform and safe terminations for pregnant women.

Then in 1977 she arrived with a flourish on the literary scene with *Monkey Grip*, her sharp-eyed, thinly disguised, fictional account of communal living, drug use and single, lovelorn mothers in inner Melbourne. And although some of her friends ended up feeling betrayed by how they'd been captured in print, the book established Helen as one of the clearest and strongest post-1960s feminist voices in Australian writing.

Since then, with the publication of various novels, essays, articles, short stories and books of reportage, her reputation has only grown. Helen is a writer who explores in lean, haunting prose the rough ground of people's lives. She employs the small canvas to paint big, broad brushstrokes about the messy, neurotic, endlessly complex nature of what it means to be human – whether that be in relation to the collapse of a marriage, the birth of a grandchild, 'the alternating rage, euphoria and stupor' of a mother's Alzheimer's disease, or, at its most extreme, the shocking death in 1990 of two-year-old Daniel Valerio at the hands of his mother's boyfriend, a story for which Helen won journalism's coveted Walkley Award.

According to publisher and friend Di Gribble, Helen's impulses are first and foremost related to honour. 'Honour is a much better word than goodness,' she says, 'because it's to do with honesty and principle and bravery, and as a reader that's the thread you always find in Helen's work.'

It is also the thread you find in Helen herself – in the way she explores the spiritual realms of existence through prayer, in the way she probes the moral dimensions of human behaviour, in the way she celebrates friendship and family.

And yet therein lies the source of a deep sadness in her – the 'failure', as she would put it, of three marriages over three decades. Never mind that her friend Di Gribble offers up the words of poet Robert Graves to explain away – in the case of the second and third marriages – these so-called failures: *Why have such scores of lovely, gifted girls married impossible men?* To Helen they are failures nonetheless.

Her first marriage, in the late 1960s, was at the age of twenty-five when she took up with Melbourne actor and writer Bill Garner, and was soon pregnant with their daughter, Alice (now a well-known Melbourne-based actor). A few years later that relationship fell apart, just as Helen was beginning to re-evaluate her life through the revolutionary lens of feminism.

Then in 1979 she fell in love in Paris with French journalist Jean-Jacques Portail. The two married the following year in Melbourne, but that partnership again proved short-lived when in 1985 it became painfully obvious that Jean-Jacques had fallen in love with Helen's youngest sister, the writer and book reviewer Catherine Ford. (Catherine and Jean-Jacques have since married and had two children.)

The undoing of this relationship became the subject for Helen's powerful screenplay, *The Last Days of Chez Nous*, one which Helen feels she might have written prematurely, given the raw and still unresolved nature of her emotions. It is a subject she understandably still tiptoes around.

'Aside from family events, I don't see him [Jean-Jacques] but I'm always pleased to see him and I think he's pleased to see me,' Helen says now, frowning slightly and doodling on a piece of paper. 'I think maybe it's more weird for them than it is for me . . . It's a strange thing to happen. And of course when it did happen it was hideously painful. I suppose it's the kind of emotional event that could really sink your ship, but I couldn't allow it to sink my ship because I had to be there for my daughter who was about to do her last year at school.

'So I think I backed a truck up to the thing and poured a very large load of concrete all over it and that was how I kind of got myself through it. But you see, that sort of stuff lies in wait for you, and the next time things go wrong emotionally, the concrete kind of gets jackhammered up, and underneath it is this seething mass of unresolved sorrow and pain.'

By the late 1980s Helen had formed a relationship with Murray Bail, author of *Homesickness*, winner of the 1980 National Book Council Award and (shared) *Age* Award. That relationship lasted until 1998, during which time Helen would publish her hugely controversial *The First Stone* and Murray would win the prestigious Miles Franklin Literary Award for his novel *Eucalyptus*.

Today, Helen offers up a barely convincing explanation for why the relationship foundered. 'I think it's hard for two writers to be married to each other,' she says softly. 'I think most writers are actually peculiar people. They are rather solitary types. To write, you have to spend an enormous amount of time by yourself. You have to endure enormous stretches of solitude. That's hard to match up with marriage because marriage involves certain intimacies . . . a certain amount of being social with the person you're married to.'

Plus, Murray Bail was a purist with a 'stern, Methodist approach' to his work and life, dismissive of nonfiction and scornful of popular culture. Helen, by contrast, was more the dilettante, prepared to turn her mind to all forms of writing in order to make a living. Also, she liked fun and, as she says now, 'Murray used to tease me about that and say, "What's so special about fun? People don't need to have fun." [But] I wanted to have fun. I wanted to dance.'

There was little fun to be had, of course, during and after the publication of *The First Stone*. This was Helen's award-winning and searingly honest account of a sexual harassment case at Melbourne University in the early 1990s. The book caused a sensation and turned her from a critically acclaimed Australian author into a household name. But this was not without its consequences.

Helen was vilified, blackballed and snubbed. People turned on her with a ferocity that had rarely been witnessed in Australian literary circles. Helen had done the unthinkable: she'd dared to side with a man, with the master of the university's Ormond College, Alan Gregory, after he'd been accused by two of his female students of indecent assault. The women claimed that Gregory had fondled their breasts at a valedictory dinner, claims which Gregory strenuously denied.

Alan Gregory was charged by the police, and eventually, on appeal, found not guilty. Nonetheless his reputation was destroyed. Helen Garner's view was that, even if he was guilty, it was nothing short of overkill to call in the police, take him to court and ruin his career and family life in the process. Whatever happened to grades of offence? she was to ask. Whatever happened to women dealing with slightly nerdish passes by inebriated men in less punitive ways? Whatever happened to the idea that male–female relationships were filled with ambiguity; so often fraught with misunderstanding?

As a result of *The First Stone*, women around Australia began re-evaluating their own experiences of inappropriate sexual behaviour. Men and women argued the merits and implications of the book long into the night. Meanwhile, Helen found herself a public figure for the first time, a status she hated. She also found herself cast as the traitor, a feminist who'd sided with the patriarchy and all its blunt instruments of power.

Not only were most of the protagonists in the book left fuming, but certain so-called friends turned their back on her at public events. Academics refused to even read the book, and one reader actually had the temerity to berate Helen's ex-husband's wife for what Helen had written.

And all through this period, Helen was becoming increasingly aware that her marriage to Murray Bail was crumbling. 'It was my third marriage,' she says now, 'and when it became clear to me that the thing was on the rocks, or it was heading for the rocks, or that there was nothing I could do to steer it off the rocks, I desperately clung on.

'I could have jumped off that ship before it hit the rocks. I don't know if I should have, but I could have . . . But I thought, "Oh no, not again, I'm so hopeless." I had this terrible sense that there was something deeply wrong with me; that once again I was about to have one of these marital smash-ups.'

And so the story of Joe Cinque landed in Helen Garner's lap at one of the darkest moments in her life. Her marriage had just unravelled and she was living alone in a rented flat in Sydney. It was all she could do to venture out into the world, as her diary would testify to:

> I go home and lie on the bed, whether it's night or day, and fall asleep. I dream great twisted sagas of abandonment, jealousy, savage revenge . . . All day I cry at the slightest thing – a person who bumps me in the street, a cloudy sky, an empty letter-box . . . in the furniture department of David Jones I am quietly and carefully mourning the end of our marriage . . . A bottomless reservoir of tears. I'll never be able to cry them all.

Throughout 1999, while finalising her divorce, Helen had brooded on the trial in Canberra, casting a meticulous eye over the proceedings, being swayed one way, then another, until she felt literally sick from trying to work out the rightness or wrongness of the arguments being presented. The story of Joe Cinque had seized her imagination and hauled her away from her own grief. But still she wasn't ready to write.

By early 2000 she had decided to move back to Melbourne to take up the role of grandmother to her daughter Alice's first child, Olive, and to help care for her aged and demented mother. But Joe Cinque wouldn't leave her alone.

> A thousand distractions came between me and Joe Cinque's story. But it was always in my mind. It billowed like a dark curtain on every breeze that blew. It was standing by the bed when I turned over in my sleep. It was waiting for me when I woke up in the morning.

As the months passed, Helen came to the realisation that the two women central to this case – Anu Singh and Madhavi Rao – were not going to talk to her. To Helen it felt like a replay of *The First Stone* when the two women central to that story had steadfastly maintained their silence, and she'd received a 'public roasting' for proceeding regardless. 'No way,' she said to herself, 'was I going back out there.'

Except she forgot to reckon with one thing. Over the past year she had come to know the Cinque family well. She'd been welcomed into their home, been given the privileges of an honoured guest – simple yet sumptuous Italian meals, rich expresso coffee and cakes, fresh soap and handtowels in the bathroom. She'd been shown the school trophies, the photograph albums. She'd sat in their living room watching videos of Joe as a scrawny youth in a pop band, and then later as a handsome young MC at a friend's wedding. She'd heard about the depression of their other son, Anthony, as a result of his brother's death. She'd stroked the cat and kissed the cheeks of her hosts and heard the story of their lives and sat quietly in the spaces that their young, handsome son had once occupied. And in so doing, she had become part of their lives. And not only that. Joe Cinque had begun to sink into the very fibre of her being. He had become part of her awareness of the world. She couldn't walk away from him.

'All I want is for my son to be acknowledged,' Maria had told Helen on the phone one day, sobbing uncontrollably when she learnt that Helen might not proceed with the book.

'That was the point,' Helen tells me now, 'where I would have been very glad not to write it. I would have liked to flee from it, but by the time I reached that point there had been a corresponding development in the mind of Maria Cinque – and that was that my interest in the story was going to help her. She needed me to tell the story.'

In 2002 Helen was offered a teaching position at the University of Newcastle – the same town the Cinque family lived in. It is tempting to say that she was now being guided back towards the Cinque family. Who knows? What is certain is that this is when the words finally began to flow onto the page. Devastating insights into the way young women like Anu Singh increasingly come to be ruled by their bodies. Stinging observations about the availability of drugs on campus and the casual indifference of a subculture, in this case a subculture of law students, to the possibility of a murder or suicide in their midst. A searing commentary, too, on power relationships and the way blithe, happy spirits – young men like Joe Cinque – can be swallowed up by 'formidable, coercive' personalities like Anu Singh. And great flourishes about the 'elasticity' of the law and its 'brutal remoteness' to ethics and morality, not to mention the intense rage felt in the community because of what is seen as appallingly light sentences for shocking crimes.

But all these themes rose to the surface of Helen Garner's text unwittingly. What was really driving her was her desire, at last, to find Joe Cinque. To write a lament for him. For two years she had pored over court transcripts and newspaper accounts of murders and criminal proceedings. She'd read authors such as Gitta Sereny, Primo Levi and Dostoevsky and realised that in the case of the latter's towering achievement, *Crime and Punishment*, the murder victims were almost invisible in the text, as if nobody had cared enough about their loss to society to write about them.

And so, in the wake of her marriage collapse, the eventual death of her mother (in 2001), and then the tragic death of her second eldest sister, Marie, from cancer (in 2003), Helen Garner's natural curiosity and empathy for the world led her, finally, in search of Joe Cinque. Freed from the responsibility of being even-handed by the refusal of both Madhavi Rao and Anu Singh to talk to her, she began to draw Joe Cinque out of the shadows, into a place where people could see him.

> What bad is there to say about a firmly brought up Italian boy who respects his parents, whom all his friends' parents adore, who works nights in a pizza shop while he's studying for his engineering degree? The sort of bloke everyone wants to MC their wedding because he's so funny and so kind? Who comes to see you when you're slaving away in your father's fruit and vegetable shop and gives you a hand to carry boxes? Who lends you one of his flippers when you've lost yours in a heavy surf? Who never once forgets to bring a birthday and Christmas and Easter present for your kid sister? Who takes your new baby son in his arms and calls him 'my little *paesan*'?

Helen Garner's Melbourne kitchen is a tableau of domestic life. A red apron hanging on a hook. A vase of tulips on the table. A cutting board and the *Age* newspaper scattered in its various sections. A view to a garden of apricot and lemon trees, as well as willow myrtles and Chinese elms – 'Nanna's backyard', as her granddaughter Olive likes to call it.

When Helen became a grandmother for the first time four years ago, and then for a second time a few months ago, she was overwhelmed by the emotions she felt. 'The word love hardly touches the sides,' she was to later write. 'At my age, you do not expect to be consumed by a passion so intense. I can't stand it when people say, "Grandchildren are wonderful!" then add, in a roguish way, "because you can give them back". I don't want to give her back. I am almost frightened by the ferocious love I feel for her.'

Helen Garner can't help herself. She writes like a dream. Put a story in her hands, any story, mundane or extreme, and it will leap from the page and drag you into its embrace.

The story of Joe Cinque lay in wait for her, biding its time before she was able to find the strength and subtlety of mind to tell it. When she finally did, she sent the finished manuscript to Nino and Maria Cinque, as a matter of courtesy, but more importantly to make sure that they recognised her portrait of their beloved son.

For two weeks Helen waited for their reply. She could barely think straight. Then Maria Cinque rang and left a phone message. 'We like the book. We think it is good,' she said without adornment or flattery. Helen Garner burst into tears of relief.

For Helen Garner there is now a kind of freedom in having written this book. It is no longer standing by the bed when she wakes in the morning. 'It's taken a big load of strain from my relationship with the Cinques,' she says finally. 'Now I don't have a feeling of frustrated responsibility towards them anymore. I just think of them as people I have grown to love and for whom I have enormous respect.'

For the Cinque family, nothing will ever bring their Joe back to them. But the fact that his story has been told, that his warmth and humanity have not been forgotten . . . well, that for them, and for Helen Garner too, might be the only consolation there will ever be.

ALISON BROINOWSKI
This Is the Way the World Ends

Alison was a guest of the Byron Bay Writers Festival in 2004.

For decades, dozens of books and movies have thrilled and chilled us by anticipating a frightening future. *On the Beach, The War of the Worlds, The Decline and Fall of Great Powers, The Day of the Triffids, The Clash of Civilisations* and *The Day After Tomorrow* are only a few of them. None of it may happen, or it may happen in part, or it may come true in a year other than the one predicted, as with *1984* and *The Crash of 79*. Or what happens may be something entirely beyond belief and prediction. 'The delusional,' American broadcaster Bill Moyers warned in March 2005, 'is no longer marginal.'[1]

But Americans, who have a developed penchant for doomsaying, were not its inventors. Long ago, wild-eyed Cassandra put her logo on the art of dire predictions. The Delphic oracle was notorious for dodgy ones which, like those of the witches in *Macbeth* and the soothsayers in *Julius Caesar*, had a way of coming true in unexpected ways. People's hair has been raised for centuries by the prospect of doom, from Virgil's circles of hell and Heironymous Bosch's tortures of the damned, to the living purgatory depicted by Goya and Picasso. We still get a laugh out of doomsayers, because the sky didn't fall when Henny Penny said it would, we weren't all 'rooned' as Hanrahan insisted, UFOs were said to have been seen but no green men landed, and the world's computers didn't all crash as believers in the Millennium Bug predicted. Still, that doesn't mean such things won't happen.

Having achieved great technological advances, Americans are all the more fearful that the genie they have let out may destroy them. The United States has used its nuclear capacity to flatten two cities, and it fears a similar fate for its own. Having stored anthrax in its arsenal, the United States is paranoid about being attacked with it. Americans are obsessed with 'social fatality', as Clifford Geertz recently called it. But when the United States became the sole superpower, Francis Fukuyama confidently asserted that the democratic system had fully evolved in America and could not be surpassed, and fellow optimist Thomas Friedman wrote of the unrivalled benefits of democracy and globalisation. With equal certainty, factual pessimist Richard Posner in *Catastrophe: Risk and Response* (OUP, 2005) and fictional thrill-peddler Michael Crichton in *State of Fear* (HarperCollins, 2005) anticipated ways in which we may bring about the global system's early demise.

Millions are frightened and excited, it seems, by the thought of what may turn out to be the Next Big Thing. Jane Caro used that title in August 2005 in the *New Matilda* for life-changing forces that become obvious only after they hit us. 'The greatest revolutionary influences,' she proposed, 'are the things that sneak up on us, [but] are currently invisible to us.' The terrorist attack of September 11, 2001 was, of course, such a Big Thing, although both Chalmers Johnson and Samuel Huntington had predicted it. The Boxing Day 2004 tsunami and the Pakistan earthquake of 2005 were entirely unforeseen. In contrast, the 'shock and awe' attack on Baghdad in March 2003 was a Big, but universally anticipated, Thing. Hurricane Katrina in 2005 did not sneak up but was tracked for days, and its effect on the people of New Orleans was anticipated long before it hit them. A widely predicted catastrophe, whether man-made or not, about which nothing is done is perhaps the most terrifying.

What Big Thing is sneaking up even now to overthrow the hegemon? What avatar slouches towards Washington to be born? Who and what will get trampled on the way? Possible Big Things, to which we are led by today's worried writers – most of them Americans – range from terrorism itself, to catastrophe, to mayhem. Let's consider them in order.

First Big Thing: Terrorism

Americans are at war with terror. It is a fight that reinforces all that they and people like them hold dear. Terrified themselves, many are enthusiastic promoters of the dread that gets out the patriotic vote and the snake oil that lubricates the hi-tech military machine. Those who are not with them (a growing number, from columnists and academics to the protesters outside the President's ranch, and now Congresspeople too) are accused of being against them. But this is not new: during the Cold War John Foster Dulles announced that the world was divided into two groups of people: the Christian anti-communists and the others. Then, the *bête noir* was a communist in Moscow or Vietnam: today it's a terrorist in Iraq, or a nuclear technologist in

Iran or North Korea. But the pattern remains the same: Americans fear those who use their own threats against them.

Foreigners in the United States make themselves unpopular by urging Americans to apply the obvious lessons of Vietnam to Iraq. A British writer in Washington, Anatol Lieven, did this when he wrote that the great tradition of critical thought in the United States has been displaced by 'an inability to re-examine certain fundamental national myths' (*America Right or Wrong: An Anatomy of American Nationalism*, OUP, 2004). Slings and arrows were also aimed at prolific Canadian writer John Ralston Saul for arguing in *On Equilibrium* (Penguin, 2002) that the West's actions made it partly responsible for September 11, something Susan Sontag and Noam Chomsky had also written. American historian Chalmers Johnson has been criticised for saying much the same for years.

Born-again President George W. Bush winks and smirks and invokes freedom, liberty and God, as if to send a coded message of reassurance to the faithful. He declared at his second inauguration: 'America's vital interests and our deepest beliefs are now one.' This evidently resonates in a fearful electorate that wants to hear that America is the greatest country on earth and the good guys are winning. Leaders can smell votes and money in religion. The politically-driven return to religious dogma is shredding the secular division of church and state, God and Caesar, and it wins elections in the United States and the United Kingdom. And, as Marion Maddox has shown, Australians copied the trend of its Anglo-allies. In the years that intervened between her two books, *God under Howard* (2005) and *For God and Country* (2001), it became more common for personal faith to be paraded in Australian parliaments. In spite of our traditional cynicism about snake oil, goanna oil and unique water, political religiosity is on the rise in Australia too. No wonder Osama bin Laden – who should know – calls us all Zionist Crusaders.

At Christmas 2004, John Howard told Parliament that Christianity was the nation's 'greatest force for good' and for the 'enhancement of individuals and the liberation of the human spirit'. Apparently un-Constitutional though this statement was, it went unquestioned in a House of Representatives where all three parties are led by professed Christians.[2] The prime minister chooses Jesus as 'the most significant figure in human history', Tony Abbott tries to stir the abortion debate, and Alexander Downer instructs the errant clergy. Peter Costello prays at the Hillsong church where believers hold that 'our eternal destination of either heaven or hell is determined by our response to the Lord Jesus Christ'.[3] Faith, it seems, is now as much the public badge of the patriot as of the fanatic. If that leads to fascism, God will, as Stendhal said, have to excuse himself for the consequences by declaring that he doesn't exist.[4]

Meanwhile, somewhere on the Afghanistan–Pakistan border, other fervent believers also mix technology, ideology, fantasy, reality and aggression in pursuit of their interests. No Luddite primitives, they expertly deploy video, the Internet, mobile phones, improvised weapons, opium and Islamic banking in the hope of heavenly rewards. Unbelievers deserve what's coming to them, say their messages; violence will be returned for violence; we are guilty of nothing; we disregard collateral damage; our way is the only way; we will keep sending this message unpredictably and repeatedly until the foreigners understand it; and 'the Jew or Christian who insults the Prophet should be killed'.[5] Islamic factions in Iraq condemn the 'farce of democracy and elections', calling polling booths 'centres of atheism'. In August 2005 Al Qaeda ordered the death of the infidel drafters of the Constitution and their supporters.

The similarity of content between their fundamentalism and the gospel according to Bush is striking. Both have held questionable elections. Both pursue their global cause with intolerant conviction, xenophobic ignorance and reckless ruthlessness. Bush claims that the advance of freedom is unstoppable and that the United States will stay in the region as long as it takes to 'overwhelm their ideology of hate'. Those who resist him say the same. Muslims baulk at the term 'terrorist' being applied to their insurgents, resistance groups and freedom fighters, whom Palestinian cleric Sheikh Muhammad Ali calls 'the spearhead of the liberation effort'. The United States equally rejects the label 'terrorist' for its attacks on Libya, Syria and Iraq and its support of Israel, because its motive, too, is freedom. There are, it appears, 'freedom-loving people' on both sides.

It is a war over unreconciled ideas of freedom. Meanwhile, debate proceeds at the United Nations about what constitutes terrorism and how to deal with it. Two broad groups of ideas emerge about what drives the terrorists: those of unilateralists and internationalists.

The first group, unilateralists, see terrorism as the straightforward result of a fanatical Islamist campaign for a universal caliphate. For a while, such observers as Christopher Hitchens, Bernard Lewis, William Shawcross and Rohan Guneratne variously extrapolated from this the theory that poverty and political oppression in Muslim countries, and the blame-displacement of the 'Arab street' onto the West, were what drove ignorant, desperate young men to do the bidding of firebrand, power-hungry clerics. They had to be stopped, because the consequences of the West's failure to do so would be too awful.

But most of the terrorists, though fervent, turned out to be neither particularly ignorant, poor, nor oppressed. In Indonesia and the Philippines, terrorist cells thrive in spite of some growth of democracy and prosperity. So the unilateralists have fallen back on seeing extreme religious indoctrination as the spur to suicide terrorism, and that it should be stopped. V. S. Naipaul argued in September 2001 that young men who wanted nothing more than a green card were paradoxically prepared to destroy the United States, and the logical response was to expel or arrest those with such views. 'Holy war for Muslims,' he said after the July 2005 attacks in London, 'is a religious war and a religious war is something you never stop fighting.'[6]

Internationalists are more eclectic about the causes of terrorism. For some who agree with Samuel Huntington, terrorism arises from a clash of Islamic culture, language and religion with those of the West. The clash observed by others, including Tariq Ali and Marise Ruthven, is one of fundamentalisms between the West and the Muslim world. Others again describe a clash within Islam, between moderates and extremists. Such a confrontation is observably building in the West too. Fundamentalism of whatever kind puts believers on a collision course with unbelievers: but it is the fundamentalists whose faith commands them to destroy the infidel who become terrorists. Their targets are identified by nationality, race and religion, and so terrorism appears to be an extreme form of xenophobia, ethnic cleansing or holy war. Because it has no logic, such a war is also 'something you never stop fighting'.

Robert Pape's painstaking research at the University of Chicago suggests that more is involved than religious zeal and xenophobia and that there can be an end to the fighting. His investigation of suicide terrorist attacks committed in many places, and not just by Muslims, revealed that, while all suicide terrorists wish to die while randomly killing as many others as possible, the 462 who killed themselves between 1980 and 2004 also shared a fierce resistance to occupation by foreigners – not just Westerners – of what they considered their territory. In fact, of those who died, more were Sri Lankan Hindu Tamils than Muslims. Professor Pape and his multilingual team analysed the sermons and writings of Islamist leaders, as well as statements by Tamil Tigers, Lebanese, Chechnyans, Kashmiris and Palestinians, in reaching their conclusions. He didn't dismiss the role of religious fundamentalism, but suicide-terrorist attacks, Pape concluded, are 'not driven by religion as much as they are by a clear strategic objective: to compel modern democracies to withdraw military forces from the territory that the terrorists view as their homeland'.[7]

So, if Pape is right, a nation becomes a target for suicide terrorism less because of its identity and more because it has an armed presence in a certain territory. Thus, for the leaders of the 'Anglosphere' (as George Monbiot calls it) to claim that the terrorists are driven by 'who we are, not what we have done' is dangerously to misunderstand their many explicit messages about their intentions. By going on fighting in Iraq, the Anglo-allies are doing exactly the opposite of what is needed to 'defeat terrorism', and are instead creating the conditions for more of it. That can only lead to the allies' eventual defeat.

The longer military occupations continue, the more people will sign up as terrorists. Offended by the US presence in the Arabian peninsula, Osama bin Laden abandoned his youthful indiscretions, adopted Salafist fundamentalism, and embarked upon a vengeful campaign of violence. This is a life-pattern that many *mujahiddeen* had followed before him, and one that many terrorists acting in his name – whether he is alive or dead – have followed since.

That Prime Minister Tony Blair failed to grasp this was demonstrated by his reaction to the London bombings. They revealed what had been thought to be impossible: that suicide terrorists could be British-born. Perhaps Blair had forgotten Richard Reid the shoe-bomber: but then he didn't attack London. British intelligence must now be factoring into their analysis of terrorism the British historical occupation of large parts of the Middle East, Britain's creation of modern Israel at the expense of the Palestinians, and its recent re-invasion of Afghanistan and Iraq. Blair was warned over a year ago, but instead of admitting that the invasion of Iraq was wrong and counterproductive, he insists it's a response to terrorism. But Pape's theory more credibly explains the urge of young Muslims to attack those whose military occupy their ancestral lands, even if they too are British.

Australia's leaders continue to copy and paste the blinkered intelligence of the Anglosphere into their public statements, adopting its 'values-based' religiosity and parroting its lies. They always claim it was our identity, not our actions, for which Australians were attacked in Bali and Jakarta. Their embedded columnists keep saying 'Yes, Minister, Bali happened before Iraq'. So it did; but the smiling Bali bombers themselves declared they targeted Australians because we were allies of the United States, had taken East Timor from Indonesia, had already invaded Afghanistan, and were about to invade Iraq. That this was Australia's intention when the terrorists blew up Kuta in October 2002 was as clear to them as it was to me, an ordinary onlooker, when I began writing *Howard's War* (Scribe, 2003) in November 2002.

A terrorist attack on Australia, according to the rational analysis of both the Australian Federal Police Commissioner and the former head of ASIO, is more likely because by invading Iraq we made Australia a larger target. It could occur this year. When it does, the unilateralists and the internationalists will divide even more sharply, as the red and blue states are divided in the United States, and as the Blair authorised version opposes the Monbiot unauthorised version of the war.[8] The same division is already evident in Australia. Muslims everywhere are united as brothers by a sense of shared alienation, as potent in Lakemba as it is in Leeds or Lebanon or Kuala Lumpur. In reaction, John Stone and Imre Saluszinsky call for all Muslims to be treated as aliens.

Stone, a former senator and a former head of Treasury, told readers of the *Australian* just after the London bombings that Australia had a 'rapidly growing Muslim problem'. He recommended halting Muslim migration and imposing punitive measures on Muslim citizens in Australia, which he often calls a 'Judaeo–Christian Western civilisation'.[9] Slightly more sophisticated, Saluszinsky quoted one of literature's maddest fascist tyrants, Conrad's Mr Kurtz in *Heart of Darkness*, as a model counter-terrorist. He urged Australia 'to "exterminate the brutes": exterminate them before they create another 100 motherless or fatherless children in Madrid or London or Melbourne'.[10] So how do we identify the brutes for extermination? Better than the British police, one hopes. What about the thousands of motherless or fatherless children in Baghdad? Are Australians in favour of their extermination too? Iraqis may well have gained that impression since 2003.

Stone and Saluszinsky are unilateralists, concerned with the impact of nations' actions on them and *their* kind of people: internationalists like Pape and Monbiot consider the impact on *all* people equally. A former Director of Central Intelligence and Deputy Secretary of Defence spoke against the war at Harvard in June 2005, but sought to reconcile these two camps. Professor John Deutch argued that US foreign policy should be guided by two principles: 'first, to advance our country's security and political interests, and second to encourage prosperity and responsive government for people around the world'.[11] Encourage, not impose: there is a difference.

In Australia as in America, the unilateralists are ascendant. It's fine to be an elite sportsperson or a millionaire talk-back host, but the twilight of intellectual elites can't come soon enough for Miranda and Frank Devine, Andrew Bolt, Janet Albrechtsen, and David Flint, who celebrated it in his 2003 book. Australians who dissent from their views are publicly demonised, and the hack-pack joins the hunt. The hue of the Sydney Institute's quarterly *Media Watch* and the cry of the shock-jocks direct the punters to the prey. At such times the best lack all conviction, as Yeats knew, while the worst are full of passionate intensity.

Predictions of a final cataclysm come in two broad groups: catastrophic destruction by foreseeable factors we have failed to prevent, and mayhem that is out of our control. Catastrophe first.

Second Big Thing: Catastrophe

Natural disasters can be foreseeable and unforeseeable. In his 2005 book, Richard Posner surveys dozens of 'acts of God', particularly extinction events outside the normal American experience, like the earth being hit by an asteroid or a sudden ice age. He specialises, however, in disasters caused by technology run wild: nuclear winter, say, or a germ-war pandemic caused by gene splicing, or a particle accelerator which, out of control, could either radically compress all matter or could create a 'strangelet' that would grow and grow and consume all matter. Posner, a US judge, wants controls clamped on everything: stronger international policing, limits on access for foreign students to the United States, curtailment of civil liberties, and requirements for scientists to demonstrate social responsibility. (Perhaps that, implying threats to their funding, explains why many American scientists are suddenly finding religion.)

Economic disasters are more often predicted than experienced, but that hasn't stopped writers from Paul Erdman in the 1970s to Warren Buffet and George Soros in the 2000s expecting them. When Erdman, having already published *The Billion Dollar Sure Thing*, wrote *The Crash of 79* in 1974, it was front-paged by *New York* magazine as 'The coming oil war: how the Shah will win the world: an all too plausible scenario'. Erdman was both wrong and right: the Shah didn't win, but Iran still might, at least in the Middle East; and war over oil remains all too plausible. Soros, in his diatribe against Bush's unilateralism, *The Bubble of American Supremacy: Correcting the Misuse of American Power* (Allen & Unwin, 2004), warned of the collapse of the world's financial trading system. He was right to seek reform of the United Nations, the World Bank and the International Monetary Fund, but his predicted collapse may well happen before reform does.

Criticisms of the chronic US deficit by Soros, Paul Volcker and others don't go nearly far enough for George Monbiot. His concern is not to save the US economy from collapse. He called in *The Age of Consent* (Harper Perennial, 2003) for the overthrow of existing institutions and their replacement by a genuinely democratic world order that would eliminate national boundaries (as Richard Falk also did at Princeton for three decades). Monbiot advocated an International Clearing Union to discharge trade deficits and prevent the accumulation of debt, and a Fair Trade Organisation to restrain the world's rich and emancipate the poor. John Ralston Saul, too, has proposed the reinvention of the world system, calling globalisation 'anti-democratic and a failed experiment' that is already in meltdown (*The Collapse of Globalism: And the Reinvention of the World*, Viking, 2005). Recently, Clyde Prestowitz has predicted a 'great shift of wealth and power to the East' in *Three Billion New Capitalists* (Basic Books, 2005). He welcomes the rise of China and India and urges Americans not to regard them as enemies, but warns that if China and Japan sell off the US dollar, economies everywhere will collapse.

Predictions of *political* disaster seem to chill readers even more than economic ones. All great powers have declined and fallen, and more often because of 'imperial overstretch' than because of defeat by a rival. Great powers, as Barbara Tuchman showed in *The March of Folly: From Troy to Vietnam* (Joseph, 1984), are eventually brought down by what in retrospect seem deliberate, wanton errors of judgment. Later in the 1980s, Paul Kennedy surveyed five centuries of these collapses in his bestseller *The Rise and Fall of the Great Powers: Economic Change and Military Conflict from 1500 to 2000* (Random House, 1987). Both wrote at a time when America could still have learnt the lessons of Vietnam. But by the 2000s, decline and fall seemed closer for the United States. Anon. (Michael Sheuer), in *Imperial Hubris: Why the West Is Losing the War on Terror* (Brassey's Inc., 2004), was one of many to foresee the calamitous political consequences of the evolving Iraq disaster. In his resignation letter to the Secretary of State, US diplomat Brady Kiesling described the administration's policies as contrary to American values and interests. 'Our current course,' he warned, 'will bring instability and danger, not security.' Chalmers Johnson shared his fear that 'we will lose our country'.

Johnson detailed the unintended consequences of American operations abroad in *Blowback: The Costs and Consequences of American Empire* (Metropolitan, 2000), warning even then of retaliatory attacks on the United States by people it had victimised. The United States, by continuing forcefully to impose democracy and free trade, spreading its military bases to scores of countries, and making itself 'a military juggernaut intent on world domination', has become a target for multiple vengeance, Johnson argued in *The Sorrows of Empire: Militarism, Secrecy, and the End of the Republic* (Verso, 2004). Forgetting what the Declaration of Independence called 'a decent respect for the opinions of mankind', the United States has developed the same unilateralism that brought down the Soviet Union. The same combination of economic contradictions, ideological rigidity, imperial overstretch, inability to reform and official disinformation, Johnson warned, will eventually produce the same result.

In the view of Niall Ferguson, a British academic at Harvard, and the author of *Colossus: The Price of America's Empire* (Penguin, 2004), the United States denies it has imperial designs, while trying to advance them in haste, on the cheap, and through proxies. Determined to dominate, it is already overstretched, and has forfeited much of the admiration it once had around the world. Writing before September 2001 and publishing afterwards, Charles A. Kupchan anticipated these developments in *The End of the American Era: US Foreign Policy and the Geopolitics of the Twenty-first Century* (Knopf, 2002), warning that stiff-necked unilateralism on the part of the United States would alienate others. The Europeans, he predicted, would pose a greater threat to American primacy than Islamic terrorists.

In what Rumsfeld scorned as 'old' Europe, many now see the United States as a less evolved society than theirs. Having put their own militaristic past behind them and concentrated on prosperity, human rights and social welfare, Europeans prefer to think Americans, not themselves, are trapped in the past: obsessed with guns, jails, drugs, debt, the death penalty, abortion struggles and gay rights debates, and stuck with inequitable working conditions, unaffordable health care, uneven education systems, struggling minorities and imperial measurement. Cosseted as the Europeans admittedly are with their protected farms, short working hours and social services, they take pride in their cooperation, justice and harmony. Europe has its share of 'new' problems too: illegal migration and hostile reactions to it, demographic Islamisation, cultural globalisation, troublesome neighbours, and public dissent about the terms of their union. Both Niall Ferguson and Timothy Garton Ash continue to hope that the Atlantic rift can be bridged for the sake of shared interests. But as more Europeans walk away from US policies, the only hands still reaching west across the ocean may be British.

Garton Ash, in *Free World: America, Europe and the Surprising Future of the West* (Random House, 2004), thinks the real weapons of mass destruction are global poverty and environmental catastrophe. With their superior aid efforts and green policies, the Europeans are ahead of the United States on both. Poverty I'll keep till last, and think here about *environmental* catastrophe. The US administration is bent on dismantling environmental protection, and ideologically determined to block mandatory international action on pollution or global warming. Not only do Americans proportionately consume more energy and raw materials than anyone else, they are also great polluters, to the extent of now increasing the risk to their own environment and health. Some 41 per cent of Americans surveyed by the Pew Centre in 2005 considered environmental activists to be 'extremists'. Christian Coalition leader Pat Robertson labels environmentalists the 'evil priests of a new paganism that will become the official state religion of the New World Order'.[12]

People living in a destroyed environment don't care about leaving it in droves. People who expect imminently to go to heaven are unlikely to care if they destroy their environment. So ideology and theology disable those who are trying to deal rationally with the growing ecological crisis. Christian Right advocacy groups don't include the environment among their 'moral values', Bill Moyers says, and they use religion as an instrument of political combat. Australian Tim Flannery and American Jared Diamond agree with British Garton Ash on the catastrophic consequences of this for the environment. Yet in what Flannery, author of *The Weather Makers: The History and Future Impact of Climate Change* (Text, 2005), calls 'a deeply troubling situation', Republicans back the energy industry and discredit the environmentalists, using 'misrepresentations and pseudoscience'.[13] Americans who swallow snake oil about the end times are strangely sceptical about the consequences of global warming.

Their refusal – with their loyal Australian followers – to accept the science, see what's coming and act in time to prevent it is Diamond's theme in *Collapse: How Societies Choose to Fail or Succeed* (New York, 2005). In all the past and present societies he studies, the single common factor determining their collapse or survival is the environment. In China, the United States and Australia, he warns, current prosperity disguises the overreach and waste that, if our ecological heedlessness and political opportunism continue unchecked, will be ruinously disastrous. And that, Australians seem to be forgetting in our rush to flog uranium, applies to nuclear power as well, which is neither clean, green nor cheap.

Third Big Thing: Mayhem

For Timothy Garton Ash, and for Jeffrey Sachs, the author of *The End of Poverty: How We Can Make It Happen in Our Lifetime* (Penguin, 2005), the poverty of two-thirds of the world's people represents as great a threat to everyone as environmental collapse. The statistics are well known. Almost half of the world's six billion people live on less than $2 a day, and one-fifth on less than $1. The United States spent $450 billion this year on the military, and only $15 billion on addressing global poverty. It has 4.5 per cent of the world's population and 20 per cent of its income, and Americans consume 25 per cent of the world's resources. The world's rich countries have a combined annual income of $30 trillion, shared between one billion people. The combined wealth of the world's ten richest people in 2002 was $266 billion: five times what rich countries spend in a year on aid for poor countries, and enough to reach all the United Nation's millennium development goals.

But those goals, reasonable and practicable as they are, will not, on current performance, be met by 2015. This is because rich countries that promise to do so won't pay up: but it's also because rich people in poor countries keep most of the aid and the proceeds of trade for themselves. Rich people in rich countries do the same. American women writers, particularly, have deplored the system for decades: they include Cheryl Payer in *The Debt Trap, the IMF and the Third World* (Penguin, 1974), Frances Moor Lappe and her colleagues in *Food First: Beyond the Myth of Scarcity* (Houghton-Mifflin, 1977) and Susan George in her many books. George's black satire of the rich world, *The Lugano Report* (Pluto, 2003) proposes to an unnamed, powerful committee how to ensure that the capitalist system is preserved in the twenty-first century. Progressing logically through the options, it reaches a final solution that George herself calls 'something really awful'. And it is. She warns of a new fascism that would include:

> ... the rule of mega-corporations, a pseudo-religious, all-embracing ideology drummed into the populace by a compliant media; mass surveillance and a master race disposing as it pleases, through military force, economic coercion or cultural bribery of the less, dark-skinned and infidel breeds, as well as the dissidents in its own ranks.

The premonitory signs of neo-fascism are evident in the final solutions proposed to Australians by Stone, Saluszinsky and the Howard government.

Resistance to it is already with us: the boat is already rocking. In Internet-linked global movements, the poor and their supporters are trying to resist big business, the banks and their client governments. Peace movements are stirring again. If enough pressure builds up, China, the Europeans and the re-socialised Latin Americans may even take a stand against US hegemony separately or, more effectively, together. The United Nations, weakened though it is, by thwarting the American administration's moves for world domination may turn out to be a catalyst of resistance. The poor have the numbers: the rich have the veto. A United States without the United Nations is what Ambassador John Bolton has said he wants: a United Nations without the United States might just be the result.

There are two kinds of people, those who believe that their ways, and their interests, are all that matter for the short future; and those who believe that the survival of all people, and our environment, matter more for the long future. Internationalists and their worldview confront unilateralists (who now include Australians, on most issues) with theirs, in their firewalled countries and gated communities. In a world without boundaries, as a senior UN official remarked, we have urgently to 'rediscover what creates the bond between humans that constitutes a community'.[14] If we don't, the end could be sooner and nastier than we think. It's not snake-oil to warn Australians to avoid catastrophe while we still have time.

ROBYN WILLIAMS
Not in Flagrante Delicto?

Robyn was a guest of the Byron Bay Writers Festival in 2002 and 2003.

I have never missed an engagement, other than a speech in Canberra. On that occasion my excuse was three cardiac arrests in one night, one of which had me flat-lined for forty-seven seconds.

In Byron, however, at my first Writers Festival, I came close. I knew I had three bookings in the big tent, but somehow a fourth had slipped past the scanner. The first I knew about it was when Festival director Jill Eddington came into our cabin at five minutes after ten on the Saturday morning saying I was 'on'. In fact the session was under way.

I was lying in bed with my partner, Jonica. We were, I'm relieved to say, merely reading the newspapers. Jill said calmly that I could make it comfortably to the venue by running across the fields – but that trousers would help. 'What's the topic?' I cried, stumbling along as I did up my fly. 'Humour in writing,' she answered.

When I got there I could see about 500 people in the marquee, already enjoying a peroration from Mungo MacCallum. I indicated my humiliation and regret by dropping on all fours and crawling past the panellists' feet, finally lifting Mungo's boot and kissing it. He accepted this as a perfectly normal tribute and continued speaking.

When it was my turn I chatted about various hoaxes I'd perpetrated, ending with one I'd written and broadcast concerning a new ABC boss 'Wayne Carey'. I said I'd chosen the name without realising someone already owned it – I'm not hot on AFL players. So my Carey became King, not so felicitous but serviceable. The scam was that I was being informed by the new management that I had to reduce the length of items on my program, *The Science Show*, from many minutes to no more than ninety seconds, to match the modern attention span, and that I would be joined as a co-presenter by a rock chick from 2JJJ who would improve my demographic. All this would be embedded in stings of rap music and other funky noises to please the kids.

My script was an interview with Wayne King, director of radio, and the role was performed on air (brilliantly!) by Felix Williamson, David and Kristin's son.

My yarn went down well with the Festival audience and I finished by remarking how disconcertingly prescient hoaxes and satire can be. A few months after the broadcast the egregious Jonathon Shier was appointed as ABC managing director and did far worse than the Wayne King of my febrile imagination. Just as I said those words I spied, standing at the back of the audience having appeared from nowhere, the new boss of ABC Radio National.

He spoke to me after the event and was charming.

Writers festivals are unpredictable. The best ones are

outside big cities where audience and speakers can spend time together and relax. In Melbourne and Sydney, however enjoyable the gigs, most of us zap in and out like visitors in a hurry. My favourites have been Byron and Norfolk Island. For once your poor book can get a little attention. Maybe the attention it deserves.

Being an author is often thankless. You come up with a presentable idea, turn it into an exciting one (you hope), labour for months (years?), lose heart, gain inspiration, become fogged, panic, are seduced then battered by your publisher – and finally receive your new shiningly bound offspring having earned not much more, when you count the time taken, than you did doing a paper round as a young teenager.

The reviews appear. Some take affront that you have dared tackle fiction. It is as if you are on some frolic. Or have farted in the lift. I am reminded of Margaret Atwood's story of meeting the brain surgeon at a cocktail party. 'Oh, you're a writer are you?' he says looking down on the diminutive author. 'Well, I've always felt I have a novel in me and I think I'll write it next summer!'

'How nice for you,' Atwood replies. 'I've always wanted to try brain surgery, and when my next vacation arrives I'll have a go.'

If you are lucky, as I have been at Byron, you'll be asked to talk about your book and give some indication of the depth of the associations, the little hooks you put out in earlier chapters not realising what they are for, stunningly finding connections for them to make thousands of words later. And the joy of hearing someone who's read the thing, and got the point, giving praise.

There are the snags: like keeping virtuously to time only to find the unblinking novelist from Melbourne running off shamelessly with all but ten minutes of the remaining time without the chair having any powers to shut her up. Or you get roped in as a universal MC and your own book is unmentioned. Or the move to the signing tent where your spot is queueless.

Then come the parties, better in Byron than anywhere else. The chance to sit with Bryce Courtney and be flattered. The opportunity to revisit Di Morrissey's lovely house and enjoy unequalled generosity. The possibility that publisher Shona Martyn might be there at the next drinks to be pumped for more gossip on Nicki Gemmell or revelations about fraudsters. Or just new friends who love books – can there be a higher form of life?

Byron Bay also *stands* for something. Like Cambridge exudes serious science and Florence *is* the Renaissance so Byron Bay for me implies artistic freedom, creativity and openness to ideas. You don't go there with sinking heart expecting some horrid pedant waiting to peck your literary liver to death.

And Byron means weather. Even if you are surprised in bed, late for your gig, I think you could get away with putting on a pair of shorts and sprinting for it. But I hope I won't get caught out again.

MELISSA LUCASHENKO
Essays and the New Journalism

Melissa has been a guest at the Byron Bay Writers Festival in 1998, 2000, 2001, 2002, 2004, 2005 and 2006. She delivered this talk at a panel addressing the subject in 2005.

I find myself a bit surprised to be here today, since I came pretty close to cancelling my sessions at this festival. I live up the road near Billinudgel, and I've got horses there, Arab horses mainly. Last Wednesday afternoon I suggested to my very beautiful young Arab mare that it might be fun to gallop bareback up to our back fence. She put to me the alternative suggestion that it would be more fun to make a very sharp right hand turn and go back to where the other horses were. So we literally went our separate ways. No one else was at home, and yelling for help was pointless, but I lay flat on my back in the paddock yodelling pretty loudly for a while before deciding that I was going to live. So if what I have to say today is a little disjointed, I apologise in advance.

Essays, why do we love them? Years ago the ABC posted a

series of celebrity profiles on its website. One of the questions everyone was asked was what their pet dislike was. The only answer I remember is that of the singer Deborah Conway, who said her pet dislike was 'Other people's certainty'. This struck a great booming chord with me when I read it. Other people's certainty.

Aboriginal people have lived a very long time with the consequences of other people's certainty. It's a truism that the outsiders who have historically come into our communities consist of the 'three Ms' – missionaries, Marxists and madmen. All three categories – which come to think of it aren't mutually exclusive – are made up of people who are very certain of what is wrong with Aboriginal people, and very certain of the ways to fix us up.

Now, I think certainty is highly regarded in most of white Australia. It's a compliment, after all, to say of someone 'he knows his own mind'. I've even heard it said, as a compliment, 'she always has something to say', as though the manufacture of opinion in Australia was somehow difficult, or rare. And the absolute inflexibility of our prime minister on certain issues is apparently a comfort to much of the population, who confuse rigidity with strength and who curiously seem to forget how utterly flexible John 'never ever' Howard can be when it is expedient to be that way.

So certainty – *sticking to your guns*, in another telling phrase – is seen as a Good Thing. But in Aboriginal Australia, certainty is usually regarded with scepticism and suspicion. The word for deafness in many Aboriginal languages is the same as the word for mental illness. In some dialects of Bundjalung you could say of someone that they are *binung goonj* – ears broken. Can't hear. Won't hear. And if any of you live with someone who is deaf and refuses to wear a hearing aid, you will have an inkling of what it has been like, historically, to be Aboriginal in Australia.

Shortly after 1788 we started saying: *We live here, this is our land.* Very few whitefellas heard it.

And around the same time we were saying: *These are our lives, and precious to us if not to you.* Very few whitefellas heard it.

And a short time after that: *These are our children we love, don't take them away.* Very few whitefellas heard it.

And continuously, ever since the invasion up till the present day, we have said: *Everything that lives is sacred, nothing is for nothing.* Very few whitefellas heard it. *Binung goonj.*

What's this got to do with essays and journalism? Well, journalists are notoriously hard-headed, hard-bitten people who drink too much because of the ugliness they've seen. As the US humourist Dave Barry puts it: 'I realise this is a bad time for you, Mrs Smith, but how did you feel when you found Mr Smith's head?' Journalists who can't hear don't last very long as journalists, but journalists who hear too well don't seem to last very long either. And this has to do with time.

For upwards of sixty thousand years, Aboriginal people were time-rich, especially in coastal areas like here in Byron Shire. Kooris were wealthy people, and Captain Cook said so of the blackfellas in Cooktown, remarking on how well we lived compared with his people back home. Plenty of food, plenty of water, plenty of time to relax, tell stories, engage in ceremonies. Plenty of time for observation. Plenty of time to learn how to really listen. Living by the seasons and not by the clock. Aboriginal children were taught then, and are still taught now, to learn by observation and this is another relic of a time-rich culture.

Questions, especially direct questions, are a timesaving device of cultures in a hurry to get somewhere. Questions belong to people who can't stick around and find out with their own eyes and ears what's going on. And, of course, questions – relying on other people's certainty, you might say – are a way of ceding your authority. To ask a question is to replace the lived experience of your own observations with somebody else's opinion. And questions are the stock-in-trade of the mainstream journalist, who has to file copy by 5 pm or whenever in order to meet the artificial deadline imposed by a 6 o'clock news bulletin, as though news ever happens in neat 24-hour chunks.

When I write for *Griffith Review*, I try to tell stories as much as answer questions. The format of the extended essay lets me, a novelist, sit back and observe, and draw some fairly slow conclusions. More importantly, it allows me to suggest rather than prescribe. I can circle a topic rather than rushing at it in a direct line; I can weave patterns of meaning and character that sit comfortably with an Indigenous sensibility. I can give voices, inevitably distorted though they are, to Aboriginal people I know and live with, and pass a version of those voices on to a wider audience.

So while I would like to think that essays are the new journalism, I fear that as the world gets faster and faster, and the Internet with its .03 second downloads makes us literally aware of time fragments of less than a second – think about that for a while! – I am afraid that essays are the leisurely indulgence of an earlier time, and that only a minority of Australians will ever sacrifice the several hours needed to enjoy a copy of *Griffith Review*. It won't stop me writing essays though. I'm not greedy – even one reader is enough for me. And anyway, even when no one is listening, and yelling for help is pointless, it can make you feel oddly better as an Aboriginal writer to nevertheless lie on your back, yodelling, until you decide you are going to live.

PETER SINGER
The Ethical Responsibilities of Writers Addressing Political Issues

Peter was a guest of the Byron Bay Writers Festival in 2003 and then in 2004 when he delivered this plenary speech on opening night.

I imagine that I've been asked to speak on this topic because of my recent book, *The President of Good and Evil: The Ethics of George W. Bush*, or perhaps my earlier *One World*. But my very first book, *Democracy and Disobedience*, was also addressing a political issue – highly current in the Vietnam War days when the book appeared – about the obligation to obey the law in a democracy. And of course *Animal Liberation* also addresses a political issue, or to put it more precisely, it sought to make what was then a complete non-issue into a political issue.

So I've got a few things to say about the responsibilities of an academic – or more specifically, a philosopher like myself – when it comes to writing about political issues. But, of course, it is not only the authors of works of nonfiction who write about political issues. Let me broaden the picture a little by mentioning some of my favourite discussions of political issues in fiction.

If you want to learn about nineteenth-century British politics – or arguably, about politics in any era – Anthony Trollope's Palliser series is a good place to start. The novels are full of questions that we still debate today. Consider Phineas Finn's difficult decision about whether to support the great Reform Bill that will abolish the 'rotten boroughs' that allow a local lord to appoint a member of the House of Commons. Finn, a young and ambitious, but penurious, member of the Commons, knows that the cause of reform is just and right. But the Reform Bill will abolish his own seat, and thus threatens to end his brief political career. He votes against his conscience and with his party. For this he is rewarded with the paid junior cabinet position of Under-Secretary for the Colonies. We can find parallels with that kind of choice today. More unusual, perhaps, is Plantagenet Palliser's decision to save his marriage rather than accept the position of Chancellor of the Exchequer, which it has long been his ambition to hold. For a contemporary version of Trollope, I recommend Joe Klein's *Primary Colors*, especially for its discussion of whether, in trying to get yourself elected, the end justifies the means.

Some works of fiction can be seen as polemical arguments for particular causes. And some of them even succeed. Harriet Beecher Stowe's *Uncle Tom's Cabin* probably did more to influence American popular opinion against slavery than any work by a nonfiction writer. Stowe achieved her objective by displaying, sometimes in tear-jerking prose, the extent of the violation of vital human interests that slavery causes. Later works like Ralph Ellison's *Invisible Man* did something similar for the racist system that prevailed in the American South during the first half of the twentieth century.

Do writers, whether of fiction or nonfiction, have special ethical responsibilities when they turn to political issues? I think they do, but since there are so many different ways of addressing political issues, it is not easy to say what these responsibilities are. But let me start with the situation I know best. What do philosophers have to contribute to the public discussion of political issues, and what responsibilities do they have?

When I was studying philosophy in the 1960s, philosophers, at least those writing in English, did not address political issues. The prevailing view of the period was that moral philosophy is quite separate from 'moralising', a task best left to preachers. What was not generally considered was whether moral philosophers could, without merely preaching, make an effective contribution to discussions of practical issues involving difficult ethical questions. Could they, by getting clear about the concepts involved, and analysing the arguments being put forward, raise the level of public debate? The value of such work began to be widely recognised only towards the end of the 1960s, when first the US civil rights movement and subsequently the Vietnam War and the rise of student activism started to draw philosophers into discussions of the moral issues of equality, justice, war, civil disobedience and, subsequently, into topics like abortion and other issues in bioethics. In these areas philosophers have, in my perhaps biased view, greatly enriched, and often elevated, the public debate.

In deciding, about two years ago, to write a book about the ethics of George W. Bush, I was motivated in part by this aim. Bush made innumerable speeches about good and evil, right and wrong, but the moral views that he was putting forward were never subjected to systematic critical scrutiny. They were either accepted as obviously right, or rejected as a blatant attempt to con the American public into believing that the president was acting from high motives, when he was really just trying to enrich his friends and cronies, especially those in the oil business. I wanted to do something different, to give the president the benefit of the doubt about his sincerity, and see whether there was a coherent ethic underlying his expressed moral views.

As I said, I was motivated in part by this aim of elevating the debate. But, to be candid, I also hoped that I might persuade a few independently minded people not to support Bush's re-election. So I can't claim to have been writing from a position of pure impartiality or detachment. But I felt that I had to keep the book honest. That meant, not merely trying very hard to get all the facts right but also acknowledging those areas in which Bush had done the right thing, or at least had come closer to doing the right thing than his predecessors. This wasn't too difficult, because I was confident that an entirely fair appraisal of the president's ethics would still leave the reader in no doubt about the fact that he lacked a coherent and consistent ethic, and that his policies frequently failed to meet even his own ethical principles.

Those of you who know my *Animal Liberation* might object that this work is more explicitly polemical than one might expect from a philosopher. That's true, in the sense that it was written from a strong sense that we humans are carrying out a great moral crime by inflicting severe and prolonged suffering on billions of sentient beings, often for quite trivial purposes of our own. I wanted to marshal every argument, and every fact that I could, in order to alert readers to what we are doing and why it is wrong. (It has been fascinating to read, in John Coetzee's *Elizabeth Costello*, a fictional portrait of a person motivated by a very similar, and perhaps even more acutely sensitive, attitude to the same ongoing atrocity.)

Does this kind of polemic transgress an important ethical boundary? Although I believe that the facts and arguments I put forward still stand up, perhaps I did slide too quickly over some objections. Certainly as a philosopher, I can see that there is more to be said.

But of course not everyone writes as a philosopher, and even those who are philosophers don't have to write only works of philosophy. In writing against the deeply held, widely accepted, rarely questioned, practice of disregarding or discounting the interests of non-human animals, there seemed little need to make the case *for* the status quo. It had all the advantages on its side anyway. In these circumstances there is a place for polemic, but readers should know that that is what they are getting.

Consider the debate about globalisation. My initial impulse, given my background with the animal movement, the Greens and generally with the Left, was to side with those who were demonstrating against the WTO in Seattle. And on several crucial points I certainly do. But when writing *One World,* I found that some of those writing on the Left were presenting simplistic arguments that seemed designed to encourage those who had already made up their minds, rather than to persuade the uncommitted. They did not seriously examine the arguments on such vital questions as, for example, whether global trade has helped the poor. There is the problem of groupthink, or going along with the herd. It can happen on the Left as well as the Right. Just as we should not support our country right or wrong, so we should not support our political party or even our friends by putting forward weak arguments and glossing over objections that we know are strong.

Here is an example from Shakespeare, one that is particularly relevant to our own situation and the debate we have been having, since the American-led attacks on Afghanistan and Iraq, over the rights and wrongs of going to war. The passage I have in mind is from *Henry V*, the scene set in the English camp the night before the battle of Agincourt. You may remember that the English army was in France, in pursuit of Henry's tenuous claim to the French throne. Now they face annihilation at the hands of a numerically superior French army. Shakespeare therefore has a problem. Henry V, the hero of his play, has taken his army into a foreign country to fight a war for a doubtful cause against a country that was not attacking his. In this war, many English soldiers are sure to die.

Shakespeare deals with this problem in a scene in which Henry, in disguise, wanders around the camp to check the morale of his soldiers before they face the foe. He meets two soldiers, one of whom says that he'd rather be up to his neck in the cold water of the Thames than here at Agincourt. Henry counters: 'Methinks I could not die anywhere so contented as in the king's company; his cause being just and his quarrel honourable.'

One of the soldiers, Williams, replies: 'That's more than we know.'

But the other, Bates, responds: 'Ay, or more than we should seek after; for we know enough, if we know we are the king's subjects: if his cause be wrong, our obedience to the king wipes the crime of it out of us.'

Williams seems to agree with this, but points out that 'if the cause be not good, the king himself hath a heavy reckoning to make, when all those legs and arms and heads, chopped off in battle, shall join together at the latter day and cry all "We died at such a place"; some swearing, some crying for a surgeon, some upon their wives left poor behind them, some upon the debts they owe, some upon their children rawly left'.

To that, Henry makes quite a lengthy speech offering a version of the doctrine of double effect – a view much employed by Catholic philosophers and theologians – that permits him to conclude that the fate of the soldiers is not really the king's responsibility. The argument is, I think, a failure, although not everyone would agree with that judgment. What I think especially noteworthy, though, is that Shakespeare should have put so complex a philosophical argument into the mouth of the king, one that lacks the dramatic tension and the poetry of the rest of the play, and cannot have been easy for his audience to absorb. He must have thought it important to raise the question of the morality of Henry's actions, and then to defend them, not only by showing Henry to be a brave and clever leader, but by showing that he has reasoned arguments on his side. But was Shakespeare influenced here by fear of criticising the kings of England, from whom his own sovereign claimed descent? If so, it would not be the only instance in the historical plays where one suspects that to be the case.

Nor, by a long shot, would it be the only instance of writers defending leaders who go to war when they should not have done so. As you know, I've been living in the United States for the past five years. It is astonishing how ready the media have been to support Bush's wars. Journalists in America are incredibly deferential to their president. Bush has never received, in America, the kind of one-on-one grilling by a seasoned, knowledgeable journalist that every Australian political leader would come to expect. When he visited Ireland recently and an Irish journalist gave him a moderately hard time, it nearly caused an international incident.

Even the proud *New York Times* has admitted that it dropped its critical guard in the lead-up to the war on Iraq, accepting stories deliberately leaked from the Pentagon as if they were hard information. Though there has now been a belated, and welcome, reassessment of the decision to go to war in Iraq, there was no real discussion of whether the war in Afghanistan was justified, and at least in the mainstream media there still has not been.

Ultimately, what is the ethical responsibility of the writer discussing these issues? I believe we should follow the argument where it leads, even at risk of personal loss or hardship. Of course, not all of us have the courage of a Solzhenitsyn or a Vaclav Havel, daring to write the truth about Stalinism, even at the cost of imprisonment and, who knows, the risk of death. Living in Australia, or the United States, the hardships we contend with are, by comparison, utterly trivial – nasty reviews, loss of readers, abusive or perhaps threatening emails. All the greater, then, the obligation to ignore them, and say what we think right. Not only philosophers but all good writers should be the enemy of complacency.

CHRISTOPHER KREMMER

American Empire: Politics and Culture in the 21st Century

Christopher delivered this lecture at the Byron Bay Writers Festival in 2003 and appeared again in 2006.

To begin with, let me apologise for the somewhat pompous title of this address. It has the feel of a panoramic television series presented by Robert Hughes, or perhaps a book that Bob Carr might read. It was chosen months ago, when the Festival organisers needed a subject with a decent shelf life to put into the program. In that respect, at least, our pompous title has served us well. The American Empire remains at the core of global debate at the dawn of the twenty-first century.

The birth of an empire is the sort of momentous event you would expect to read about in headlines. But the new American Empire, born in the ruins of the Twin Towers, Afghanistan and Iraq, has yet to be formally announced. This may be due to the child's uncertain paternity; George W. Bush and Osama bin Laden can both credibly claim to be the father. Conservatives are in denial, but their neo-conservative siblings celebrate the birth of this lusty infant, believing it will make the world a better place – for them.

Like most epochal events, this one was prophesied. In 1997 the 'Project for a New American Century' – whose signatories include US Vice-President Dick Cheney and Defence Secretary Donald Rumsfeld – outlined an unfashionable vision of a new America based on 'military strength and moral clarity . . . to build on the successes of this past century and to ensure our security and our greatness in the next'. That word 'greatness' should have given us all a clue. But their Messiah – Bush the Second – when he finally arrived, sowed an almost millenarian fear among both friends and foes. Instead of moral clarity, he initially showed signs of hesitancy and isolationism, doubting the merits of his predecessor's proactive foreign policy, and questioning the value of American efforts at nation-building abroad.

On September 11, 2001, a Great Devil arose in the east, and the rest is History. Since then, Mr Bush has fulfilled the Cheney–Rumsfeld prophecy by expanding America's military presence in the Middle East and Central Asia, toppling regimes that defy the United States and abrogating treaties that committed it to international cooperation across a wide range of fields, from nuclear restraint to protecting the environment. Osama bin Laden is, no doubt, an unsavoury character, but he's a far from satisfactory excuse for such bad policies. Nor is that great Bushism – 'You are either with us or against us' – a useful mantra for managing a complex world.

Osama bin Laden and his band of evil men have become the justification for the smashing of civil liberties in America and allied countries, and the use of torture abroad. Military rulers like General Musharraf in Pakistan have become our trusted allies, just as Islamic extremists fighting the Soviets in Afghanistan were once billed as freedom fighters, and given three billion dollars worth of weapons and training by the United States, not to mention what Saudi Arabia gave. Then a small group of mainly Saudi extremists crashes two planes into New York, killing some 3,000 innocent civilians, and we are supposed to forget how it all came about and focus exclusively on our 'new' enemy.

But back to the empire. Travelling by road across eastern Afghanistan in the days after the fall of the Taliban in late 2001, I would occasionally notice, in the skies overhead, the vapour trails of United States Air Force B-52 bombers. One wrong move on my part – or a wrong piece of intelligence on theirs – and the flying fortresses could obliterate you. America owns the skies, just as Brittania once ruled the waves. As Gore Vidal and other writers more eminent than myself have rightly said, we live in the Age of American Empire – military, economic, diplomatic and cultural. The United States can project its power to all corners of the earth and even into outer space without the rest of the world ganging up to stop it. Just as its bombers inspired fear in me, travelling the lonely roads of Afghanistan, so too its power inspires justifiable fear among innocent people, as well as 'evil doers'.

As of last month, according to the respected GlobalSecurity.org website, 368,000 American troops were deployed overseas in some 130 countries, including nineteen of the US Army's thirty-one combat brigades. That's the equivalent of fourteen entire Australian regular armies for overseas deployment. The majority are not actively engaged in combat, but more of a holding operation, preventing changes to the status quo in regions considered vital to America's national interest. Are they a kind of Roman legion of the twenty-first century? Or a firm hand guiding our world helpfully towards what used to be called 'Truth, Justice, and the American Way'?

Strictly speaking, there is no American Empire because the president is not head of state of any country other than the United States. The term 'empire' comes from the Latin *imperium*, meaning 'absolute authority'. These days it refers to a range of differing territories brought under a single sovereignty by a foreign power. On that definition the British Empire still exists because Queen Elizabeth II is still, remarkably, Australia's head of state. But that's another debate.

It's often said that America is a reluctant empire. That it wishes not to understand the world, only to insulate itself from it. It's an important distinction that reminds us that the United States, compared with many past empires, can be relatively benign, depending on your point of view. But any empire, even one maintained for protecting a free people's security, is still an empire, representing the culture and interests of the emperor.

Imperial thinking permeates America's foreign policy, especially in the Middle East. In 1979 the US Joint Chiefs of Staff formally declared the key strategic objectives in the region. They were:

1. To assure continued access to petroleum resources
2. To prevent the rise of any local hegemony (any Arab leader who could unite or dominate the region, and thereby threaten US interests)
3. To assure the survival of Israel

These three imperatives continue to underpin US policy, which seeks political control, by resort to military force if needed, to guarantee its access to oil.

America is not, as those loyal to it maintain, reluctant to dominate the world. It is merely reluctant to take full responsibility for its colonies. It prefers swift interventions to install 'friendly governments' who can protect US interests by proxy. As we are now seeing in Afghanistan and Iraq, America is good at removing regimes it doesn't like. It is not good at replacing them with anything better, or even anything coherent. Because of this fact, America's recent military interventions fail the test of the Morality of Consequences. If you can't fix it, don't break it. Or, as the Scottish historian Niall Ferguson puts it, if we cannot rebuild the nations we have defeated, we should not invade them. Bullying and manipulation, rather than consensus building, has been the hallmark of American foreign policy under George W. Bush. And it hasn't worked. The best kind of power doesn't always need to demonstrate its potency. China has nuclear weapons, but it has yet to attack anyone else with them.

As an empire, the United States behaves pretty much like other empires in the past, especially when it comes to adventures in the Middle East. History may yet compare George W. Bush with Napoleon Bonaparte. In 1798, inspired by the conquests of Alexander the Great 2,000 years earlier, Napoleon set out for Egypt. French spin said that the mission's aim was to liberate the Egyptian peasantry from the tyrannical Mamluks, to respect Islam, and to restore the Egyptian economy. In fact, Napoleon was acting on the advice of Tallyrand that a successful invasion would disrupt Britain's lucrative trade with India and the Far East. The invasion succeeded, but, harassed by the Ottomans and local *jihadis*, Napoleon was unable to establish a coherent administration. He declared victory, and got the hell out of there. I imagine a similar thing will happen in Iraq.

That example illustrates the fact that governments act in remarkably similar ways despite the passage of time and differences in religion, culture and political systems. The Cold War saw Soviet totalitarian communism pitted against American democratic capitalism, but there was no discernible difference in the tactics they employed – principally propaganda, diplomacy and the use of force. The United States prevailed, due more to the power of its economy than the power of its ideals. Individual liberty triumphed over collective solidarity, and I'd guess that for most of us here today, that was a good thing.

But history is restless. Yesterday's triumphs provide cold comfort in the face of today's challenges. Old friends become new enemies.

Like all empires, America's creates an umbrella of security and prosperity for those who share its values. Since World War II, Australia has taken shelter under the American security blanket, preferring its hegemony to the demonstrated threat of an invasion from Asia. The peace that exists in Afghanistan today – imperfect as it is, but an improvement certainly after twenty years of war – is a Pax Americana that Afghans opposed to the Taliban support. But the war in Iraq is a very different matter. It lacks both legitimacy and rationale. It's an emblem of vainglory and a reactionary view of the world that one usually associates with older, failing empires.

It's amazing to recall how briefly hope flickered in the aftermath of the Cold War that the world might escape this vicious cycle of rivalry, brinkmanship and eternal war and tension. With the Soviets gone, freedom and international cooperation were going to be the order of the day. The political scientist Francis Fukuyama declared the end of History (prematurely as it turned out) as the end of Soviet power triggered upheavals in different parts of the world. Saddam Hussein invaded Kuwait, hoping to establish himself as the undisputed leader of the Arab world, and the Balkans reverted to medieval barbarism as it tried to reorder itself along ethnic and religious lines. Freedom did not replace communism; nationalisms did, often cloaking themselves in a religious idiom for the sake of legitimacy. From global defender of capitalism and liberal democracy, America became a kind of global cop.

History tells us that empires rise and fall. If, as it seems, we are seeing the birth of an American Empire, how long will it last?

There are certain trends that suggest that a Soviet Union–style disparity is developing between US military and economic power. The United States accounted for 29 per cent of the world's production in 1950, but for only 21 per cent of global production in 1990. The economy of the rival power in East Asia, the People's Republic of China, has grown to about half the size of the United States', and is now larger than Japan's.

Nevertheless, some disastrous miscalculation aside, America will remain the world's dominant economic and military power in our lifetimes. Its longevity is bolstered by certain unique advantages. As a continental nation it cannot be invaded by land (unless Canada and Mexico fall first to its enemies). It currently possesses more than 10,000 nuclear warheads, enough to destroy the entire planet many times over. Anyone who wants to take them down will be taken down with them.

The only people who really want to destroy the United States – the Islamic militant movement – don't have the power to do so, which rather points out the exaggerated stature accorded to that particular threat by the Bush administration. It will take more than a few dirty bombs or some anthrax letters to destroy America.

We all know that the United States has, at various times in its history, provided great leadership in the world. Now is not such a time. There are instead serious questions as to the legitimacy of American power, as exercised under the Bush administration. After Iraq, the silence from the Europeans is deafening. Countries like India who have been urged to send their troops to die in 'peacekeeping' missions in Iraq have refused. In Britain and Australia there is a sordid, 'morning after' feeling of having done the wild thing after being schmoozed with pretty lies about weapons of mass destruction. The West is divided over Bush's foreign policy.

If we are indeed embarking on a century of American empire, as opposed to a merely American century, then one thing is certain: the empire will be televised. What plays well in Chicago does not necessarily play well in Cairo. When a senior American official like Colin Powell describes a vanquished Iraqi, Arab, Muslim leader like Saddam Hussein as 'a piece of trash waiting to be collected' – as he did last week – the statement is read differently in different parts of the world. From the coffee houses of Syria to the pubs of Tasmania, the global media will lay bare the emperor's every move, before a deeply opinionated global audience. And as the proliferation of nuclear technology empowers enemies and potential allies alike, the realisation will slowly dawn that even America needs friends to rule the world. For all of us, it is probably best if this realisation dawns slowly rather than suddenly.

In a world where Americans form only a small minority, their massive wealth is creating increasing envy, their arrogance increasing anger. No fortress wall can completely insulate the United States from the impact of this disaffection. In a recent article in *Esquire* magazine, Professor Thomas Barnett of the US Naval War College wrote of 'The Pentagon's New Map' which divides the world between a functioning core of globalisation and a non-functioning gap. 'Think about it,' Professor Barnett wrote. 'Bin Laden and Al Qaeda are pure products of the gap – in effect, its most violent feedback to the core.'

Will the US response to Bin Laden ameliorate or exacerbate chaos in the twenty-first century? So far, the record is discouraging. As currently conceived and executed, the discredited War on Terror will likely provoke more chaos than Muslim militants could ever have achieved on their own. Without a broader, longer-term vision of forging harmony between the world's civilisations, and recognising their just claims to their place in the sun, the billions of dollars being poured into chasing individual militants will disappear in the quicksand of Middle East and Central Asian anarchy.

Millions of ordinary Americans, let alone others, had hoped that Bush would live up to the real challenges posed by September 11. Instead, a generation of geriatric Dr Strangeloves, like Dick Cheney and Donald Rumsfeld, has hijacked America's response, just as surely as those Muslim suicide terrorists hijacked America's aircraft and smashed them into the Twin Towers. The extremists on both sides are shaping the world we live in. Their world is a dark one with a terrorist under every palm tree, and no exit strategy in the war against him. We enter the twenty-first century with America building a network of Potemkin-ised regimes, a modern version of the cantonments that once garrisoned British interests in Central Asia and the Middle East.

Yet the effort is half-baked. In Afghanistan, Hamid Karzai – a man with not just a wonderful wardrobe but a decent vision for his country – has been left stranded ever since the Iraqi adventure. His government is being kept on a drip feed of international aid – enough to survive but not to entrench a new deal for a long-suffering people.

Meanwhile, in Pakistan the United States is investing billions of dollars in the military regime of General Pervez Musharraf, while that same government trades nuclear technology with North Korea. This, while just a few hours' drive from Musharraf's home Osama bin Laden is entrenched in Pakistan's North-West Frontier Province, with what the *Spectator* magazine recently called the nucleus of another Taliban-style regime coalescing around him. By marginalising Pakistan's traditional political parties, Musharraf has paved the way for political Islam to fill the vacuum. When Musharraf eventually goes, the extremists will be well placed to take over, inheriting a small but deadly nuclear arsenal.

Domestic political compulsions are driving much of this. Bush wants to convey the impression that he is doing everything humanly possible to protect America. He fears being blamed for negligence should terrorists mount another spectacularly successful attack. But his short-sighted policies condemn future US presidents to pour trillions of dollars into new weaponry, while cutting back what little social spending is left in that country; this, in a world where America faces no credible military threat.

As I speak, American diplomats are hard at work dismantling agreements that once bound their nation in a web of mutual obligations with the rest of the world. From Kyoto to the Anti-Ballistic Missile Treaty and the International Criminal Court, every treaty has or will be re-negotiated to reduce their obligations and increase our commitments. Those who don't challenge them – like Australia under the Howard government – will be expected to take charge of their regions, deputy sheriffs patrolling the badlands. Australia's armed forces haven't been this busy for a long time.

The Bush administration's preference for guns over butter means that forty million Americans have no health insurance whatsoever. In Australia, too, increased military spending will reduce Canberra's ability to fund health, education and environment programs across the board. Australian society, and other societies that board Bush's ship of fools, will be remodelled in America's image. We will become less fair, more divided, more militaristic societies, outposts of America's Wild West Empire.

How multiculturalism will survive in such a septic environment is anyone's guess. We may find that it morphs back towards assimilation. Imagine trying to remember what we were like before becoming the more interesting nation that we are, in order to go back there. I can foresee a heavily qualified form of tolerance that forces migrants who happen to wear turbans to choose between their adopted nation and their culture. A presumption of guilt already applies to swarthy people, as the neo-conservative ratbag Ann Coulter describes them. But intolerance, if allowed to spread, will not be confined to relations between Islam and the rest. It will create a general climate of bigotry, which will strain relations between all races and religions.

Which is exactly what Osama bin Laden wants.

History will judge that America failed to define the nature of its new empire when it had the opportunity to do it, after the end of the Cold War. They allowed Bin Laden to define it for them. The American emperor concentrated on settling a personal score with the leader of Iraq, whose potential to threaten his neighbours and US interests he exaggerated. And at the end of it all, what have we got? A strange, troubled empire, whose citizens know no security, whether at home or abroad.

ROGER McDONALD
The Slim Find

Roger was a guest of the Byron Bay Writers Festival in 1998, 2002 and 2006.

Greg Johnson stopped his car at a windswept crossroads and made a call he resented making. It was to a ranger at Metro Water, and he asked – Greg Johnson, once intrinsically of those parts – asked, requested (almost cravenly begged) consent to park his car at a padlocked gate and walk to a deserted location. Lilyfield.

'We don't normally allow access,' came the disembodied voice back at HQ.

But this was Greg, mate, Greggo J. He didn't have germs on his shoes.

'What's your name again?' the official asked.

A trace of suspicion matching Greg's own suspicion of his share of reality came over.

'Johnson.'

'Don't know you, fella. You're from before my time?'

'Righty right. I'm a relic, a leftover, a dinosaur. Lilyfield used to be mine.'

A slight pause then.

'Okay. Phone me again on the way out.'

'Shall do.'

Greg palmed the phone into the glove box and nosed north along the dusty, rutty, rarely used Lilyfield road. It was busier in the past when Greg came burning down, averting head-ons on blind crests with his kids, boy and girl, screaming in the back, belting each other around the ears with their schoolbags. Now he crept along in memory, tracking the grey-day landscape in a battered Honda Civic, a scroll of dust flattening behind, limp grey formerly golden hair tousled in the wind, washed-out eyes narrowed.

It had taken Greg some years to make the return promised himself since he couldn't remember when. No planning involved, just this hung left at the crossroads when he followed the tilted signpost on a whim. All other times through the severed years he'd gone straight on past, hundreds of whistling-bys with a no thanks, another time'll do.

Arriving at the highest ridgeline the road ribboned ahead, empty and ghostly familiar. No trees. Fold after fold of dry gullies. The brilliant light made dances of eye jelly; Greg reached for his shades. A whole life lived here once. A summary of existence to slither the gravel. Was it Greg or the life lived doing the skids? Greg's hunch said the life, while those inclined to find fault blamed Greg.

He placed in a separate category of angles the sight of the Trout River catchment from the air. At one thousand feet, trimmed level after dumping super, tracking past Lilyfield heading for Mt Stony, Greg habitually glanced down on the house he then owned, gaunt paddocks and a carpet of pines along the creek, the old meat-house like a matchbox where carcases hung in winter, cased in fat for a week, colder than any fridge. The frost hollow shaded purple always told Greg there were eighteen minutes left till set-down on the Mt Stony strip, and God help him if a ground mist came in.

Dunno why, the thought always made him smile. Pancaking with the motor in cough, the prop jerked vertical. Now he'd never fly again. Too risky-disky on the ticker.

Large-knuckled hands on the steering wheel, quick glance in the rearview mirror – seeing himself, Greggo, hello – the inner voice playing mental radio, bits of old songs nasally hummed, conversations with a blowfly he couldn't get out of the car or his head.

'Who are you? You are my sunshine, my only sunshine' – thwack!

The Honda swerved on the dry grass verges, and leaning from the window Greg followed energetic gyrations of galahs coiling and sweeping a fenceline, making cries of chittery music before they flipped and went.

'Come back, return, I'm yours, I promise, goodbye.'

Where did that radio voice come from, apparently dictating existence? The ghost of himself talking it was. He re-engaged gear and drove on. Talking to that fellow back there certainly had the feeling. So this was to be the ghost day, huh, of haunt and poke about?

Hoo hoo. Too true. But –

'Too solid, my friend, you are,' Greg told himself. The contours of rocky hills and broken clay cuttings and their rough beauty were part of him. Ditto the yellowed grass the pelt of a lion. Mentally Greg reached for morning mists and pannikins of tea awaiting the sun's melt-off. There behind the hangar he stood emptying his bladder into the shaggily frosted gullies.

Everything in a man's existence took him by surprise. Just by a shift of alignment you were not where you were in space and time. Best moments came when you stumbled upon yourself accidentally complete. If life had a purpose, was this it?

Maybe that's why a crash, a charred dab in a golden paddock, had seemed the best awaiting Greg, an enlarged full stop. Then there would have been no way to say he was somewhere he wasn't, or someone he wasn't.

The crash came, but it wasn't the flying sort. Jackie handled a non-flying crash better than Greg because it wasn't a tease of imagination or dirty fuel or metal fatigue, but an emotional life event – whereas Greg thought better the bureau of air safety than a lawyer's office, the marriage counsellor's and the certified shrink's.

Greg was ageing by the calendar's reckoning and felt it in his bones. Although not too much yet, just a painful knee, a sore shoulder, a stiff neck creaking and catching when he turned his head too far. Ticker in the danger zone, however, and Greg didn't think about that, nor of his hands trembling when he lifted a coffee cup to supercharge waking. Lately single malt was his comfort, a pure refined version of heathland for someone homesick for unreachable heights.

Clouds raced over blue and hectic. It was dry, always dry out that way, but cloudy with a buffeting wind. So many crosswind landings wrestled and won. They said Greg could land backwards on a skewed arse hair.

Old emotions ran high – couldn't fight 'em. Run was the oldtime answer. Veils and curtains of a miserable day – drag them aside!

Scuds of drought vapour formed over low hills, granite boulders, thistle-beds and dead trees. There was a whole twenty-four months once when rain was condensed mist droplets and dust. Sandhills blocked the road and Lilyfield got six inches, arid zone totals. That was the year Greg stared at the sky from the end of a crowbar and Jac went to work cleaning the toilet block in the Trout Junction caravan park.

'Here we go, buddy-boy.'

A dull brass padlock and a heavy chain around a gatepost symbolised it all.

Greg parked, walked a few paces, clambered over the gate and thump landed on the other side in a bare, bare paddock. He'd seen a bloke send his thigh bone into his pelvis doing that. The track, re-routed years ago, no longer entered the old way to reveal the sweep of the landholding – a matter of joy when Greg and Jackie bought Lilyfield from the front gate. That was on the 17th of October one year, after spring rain – well-known as the mugs' date for rural real estate in the Trout catchment, poplars smelling of honey, clover frothing and rye grass imprinting rivers of wind. Lambs were almost grown out, their mothers in a grandmother mood and unfrightened. Now Greg sneaked in like a thief alarming staggy wethers.

He shaded his eyes and realised there was more than three kilometres to walk before he even joined with the old track. Because from this way in Greg could not see the shearing shed under the bark-peeling gum tree and the various improved paddocks once revealed from an elevated angle as workable and worth the price. Those dreams that were no longer on show, for which Greg had busted a gut to pay, grading a strip on the ridge above the house and building a hangar with the words Greg-Go Aviation painted on galvo ribs.

The homestead never showed itself until the last moment ever. So he didn't expect it yet. But what puzzled Greg was a plantation of pines wedged across the middle distance and showing a stiff green wall of treetops at the top of a rise as he walked along. He could not remember for a minute which paddock he was in – a neighbour's? There weren't any left. They were sold out to Metro Water and leased to sheep-grubbers until the dam was built, nobody knew when.

Greg's navigational sense was better in the air than in walking shoes. The track, upon which he trudged, sliced east between granite tors casting sheets of speckled exfoliation. In crevices safe from stock a leaseholder had jammed rolls of barbed wire. They were surely taken from a demolished fence that Greggo built with his own bare hands. But which way had it run? Even he could not tell.

And the pines, those pines – he came back to them – who planted them?

Of course, now that he thought himself into spatial order and mentally joined new track to old, he realised he did. Greg himself had planted those pines, last seen in driving rain with thousands of feathery-topped seedlings unloaded from a tractor trailer. He turned into an alleyway of trees where the trunks were solid and wild cattle lay on beds of brown needles under a canopy sheltered from wind.

Things were quiet at the creek crossing where traffic and dogs once splashed through. There came Greg taller than a shadow.

It was so quiet at the crossing now. A wombat had set up residence, burrowing under a chunk of reinforced concrete loosened in a flood Greg remembered. Milk chocolate water churned to foam, sky reduced to a torrent on flattened, wetted grass. The pump shed he built the year Polly was born still stood, ditto old tin sheets lying in a ditch, which he'd always meant to move. It was a shabbier, more condensed, grittier and a more unpleasant place than he remembered, for it was leached of Greg with a feeling of wasteland stumbled upon.

Yet here was the house, unoccupied, falling in, and the question stormed as Greg stepped up to a bedroom window with a flap of torn insect screen scratching in the wind.

Who was this being standing so intently still as to feel himself disappear?

Greg loved entering that gauzed front bedroom and closing the door against houselights, standing with his nose to the window netting and watching freeze-frames of lightning in the dark.

'Greg?' her voice called him.

A thunderclap he pretended he didn't hear. He was a youngish man in that phase of his unfolding, in which he was spared knowing the shambling rock of his sixties. The rolling plateau of granite tors and windblown tussocks gave him a sense of being alone on the planet. He liked that, and never wondered why, or what it would lead to.

Out of the darkness came the rumble of hooves. A strike of white fire and Jackie's mare skidded flashbulbed where Greg started scooping a dam before his dozer threw its tracks. In the next loud crack Cosma came at the gallop between trunks of glistening snow gums – seemingly motionless, tail erect, loudly snorting. It meant there was a gate left open or a gate knocked open in the squall. No point in rushing out, nothing to be done, but Greg hoped the mare wouldn't spike herself on a Telecom marker post he'd meant to remove. Should have yesterday, or really a week ago when the cable layers finished and Greg took them beers, a carton of Tooheys hefted high.

Back in the town of his birth Greg had been a boy standing at the window of an electrical store looking at the blank screen of a television set before he'd ever seen a TV picture. Fragments of streetlights and passing cars had the excitement of a good flick.

Jackie opened the door behind him admitting a shaft of light.

'Greg, are you in there? I wish you'd answer me. The kids are frightened and asking where you are. Don't be strange when you're needed.'

Strange. That word in Jackie's jargon meant something. She used it when he took jobs away from home. Unavailable was the other word. It was taken from a book about men and she used it to hobble him, he countered. Whereas unavailable in Greg's idea meant something huge – appetite defined as really strange and beyond his understanding. Why Jac with her beautiful wisdom would need any book raised a tricky question, troublemaking, a bad sign between them.

'Cosma's in the home paddock,' he said.

'I'm more worried about the kids just now.'

'She's your horse. But there's that steel post, y'know.'

Her silence told him she knew all about the steel post. A lesser woman would have rolled her eyes, but Jac had this implacable way, she made a monument to justice and stood there waiting. Somehow she knew the horse was safe while at the same time he was already responsible for its death.

There was a dull flash, an echo of weak thunder. The storm had moved too far away to be interesting. Greg led the way back to the kitchen.

'You can't just disappear. It's tea-time.'

Couldn't say it, having made a promise to lapse his commercials, but during a storm he was up there with his wings flung around. She knew it, though, once calling him her bird man, expecting dunno what from his need to soar – abundance?

Though what she loved in him first she blamed him for later. That was the mystery of marriage and it beat them.

'The kids are okay,' he said before they went in. 'It's you

who's frightened, Jac. You don't like saying what rattles you, that's the pits. And they pick it up.'

Sometimes Greg's explanations were only too elementary. He felt the blockiness of himself against her complications, which were all about making things simpler.

'Rattled, scared, you can say that again,' she allowed.

But brave too – with the fatalism of a soldier, he had to acknowledge. He wasn't as brave as that himself. Jac never missed a parent–teacher night and would visit old people in hospital, those she'd met at her humble jobs, or on the road befriended when their cars broke down, stuck by their steaming radiators with reptile calm. She lent money to people in trouble and gave too much, cutting the household back to neck chops and suchlike, and it seemed to please her, that Greg and the kids risked breaking their teeth on bone fragments.

Jackie's father, Frank Hinch, had been a tough old bastard. He took her from school and used her roo shooting as a kid at Byrock, where they'd kept a refrigerated trailer, insisting she aim the spot while he took them out – big reds and fully grown greys – a nightly killing for pet food suppliers until the day came when Jackie stood up to old Frank and she rocketed from home.

She'd missed so much school and was too proud to say what she didn't know. All her reading was about catching up. She still shot for the dogs, though, drawing a bead in the creek paddock at twilight, going forward with the skinning knife. He'd find her kneeling splashed with blood, hacking through sinew, because old Frank had started something that might be described as a battle against whatever it was that limited a woman.

Greg knew her secret and it confounded him. Unlike other people, who were good at shutting things off, Jac had no way of stopping what started in her head. She had to give it a proper life. Frank had behaved towards Jac as he might to a son, and that was all right, lots of girls rose to the tomboy expectation in the bush and it made them. But Jac made it an attitude about everything. She just had to do it.

'We cannot, will not, are not seeking another cent from the bank,' she'd said, when Greg came to her with the scheme for the interest-only loan that would set them back on their feet. A French bank too, which seemed a cracker of an idea to him – Banque Nationale de Paris. They were the best rates on offer. Bon chance or whatever.

A grave woman, in short. There was medication in the pantry and Jac used it, but she liked the fags and vodka greyhounds best, two or three biggies at the end of the day, and sat for hours when the kids were asleep with a library book in her lap or just listening to music on the crackly radio.

Bloody tense, that meant, at the work of living. Greg loved that dark-eyed tiredness of hers, with the downturned smile and the prominent vein in her forehead that swelled sometimes, and the bare curve of her neck which he stroked while holding her, calming her, getting her to trust him again and twisting her hair and coiling it to the top of her head.

'Nice, nice,' she'd murmur.

'I want a chance to make you happy.'

'Oh?'

These words Greg used when he first loved her. She gave him that chance. Then they were living it. Too hard but now.

In the kitchen Jackie took Polly's braids and made them tight as licorice twists. Polly was seven, precursor of wide-foreheaded beauty, holding her feelings glassily open, which meant an element of judgment visible in her mother's favour. Kim had a pale, five-year-old freckled country-boy face and he and Greg were like two dented dusty scones, the pair of them. Already they had a conspiracy of blokes, Jac said.

When Greg entered the kitchen the kids were eating their baked beans on toast with mounds of steamed spinach on the side, sprinkled with grated cheese. They had white moustaches from drinking milk and Greg tousled their hair with one hand on each submissive, grateful head.

'Don't you know you're safe in the house? It's your castle,' he said.

'The light bulb went on and off,' said Polly. 'It sort of sizzled.'

'That's normal,' said Greg.

'She said it was going to blast,' said Kim, looking up defiantly.

'That would never, ever happen,' said Greg.

They got it from Jackie, he thought. She was unable to touch a slack power-cord unplugged from a wall without wondering if it still had electricity in it. Old Frank covered every practicality in her education except her mind. They'd only had Tilley lamps out West.

Greg said: 'I saw a fireball once.'

'Not now,' warned Jackie.

'Hey, but it was quite something. It was down on the coast. Came through the lounge window and danced round the kitchen soft as fairy floss. Everyone laughed, but their hair stood on end and their fingertips glowed purple.'

'Did it blow up?' said Kim.

'I just said what it was – harmless.'

After they cleaned their teeth they went to Jackie for a story.

Greg stepped to the door and reported a clear sky.

'The stars are out. Here comes Mr Moon. Hey, Kimmy, let's go to the top of the hill and check that horse.'

'Can I, Mum?'

'Fine,' sighed Jackie, releasing an arm from around her boy's waist. He ran to Greg and launched himself at him, and Greg swifted him to his shoulders.

They walked up the hill and the mare came from shadows and followed through the gate.

The boy smelled of damp grass and fresh wind, muddy earth and a whiff of horse from stroking Cosma. The very essence of Greg he was. No way to see him as a semiprofessional League player with a head like a concrete potato, one who slips Greg cash, two or three hunnerd dollar notes at a time, withholding condemnation. Ghosts have power but only in the shape of chronology shredded, looking back, and never to the letter of outlines projected.

Later that night Jackie told Greg she didn't like him interrupting their story time. Polly was a great little reader and Kim wouldn't get hooked if Greg kept tempting him off.

'It's important a kid goes free,' said Greg.

'Whatever that means,' said Jackie. She rolled over.

'Give me my bedtime treat,' she sighed.

Greg stroked Jackie's back until he heard her quietly breathing, then turned his back to her, looked out the window into the sparkling, rain-washed night. He imagined he was a battle-tank commander. The enemy came from the direction of town. Greg had them bailed up in a gully of rocks. Tracer bullets lit the sky and he picked off small dark scurrying figures as they scattered.

One day Greg rang home and heard his own voice on the answering machine. Leaving himself a message he knew he'd be first back to savour its curiosity.

That was the day he knew he needed to run. He didn't like who he heard – 'You're goanna to die,' he told himself, so many parts of himself flown, so much unfinished.

Now, back in his ghost day, Greg goes to a high hilltop, outlook wide. The ruined house below him dreams of buckled tin. Dusk never far off in the sparkling winter light, he makes a small fire of bark and twigs among the rocks above the house before the time comes and he will have to face retracing his authorised steps to his car. He can see the car parked away and away, and knows it will be star-dark before he stumbles back to it. On the main highway fifteen kilometres away cars already have their headlights on, so far off that as the minutes pass their lights go piling into each other in a continuous animated pulp.

Once before there was something like it, along a pipeline big enough for a monkey's motorbike to ride through travelling two thousand kilometres into mountain gullies from a gasfield under the inland sky.

Greg had known nothing about it until he stumbled upon it. Taking a long back road out of ample curiosity he took a wrong turn and went for miles in the direction of sunset over bare hills. In a cleft of the dividing range had appeared that shine like a bucket of jewels.

Almost on dark it was a camp of a sort Greg had never seen before – boom gates and mesh trackways leading between brightly lit bunkrooms. A million bucks minimum in transportable comforts, there was no other way of describing it, especially to Jac, that expressed his decision fully, that there was money in this. Thus did a man immerse himself in a new dimension of revelation apologised for as a living.

It was one of those infrastructure projects you didn't read about in the papers any more, but were bigger concerns than they ever were. When Greg was a kid they were launched by prime ministers and relayed on national radio while explosives plungers were pushed and the earth shook. Now they were only written up in the financial pages. It was like receiving what he never counted on, but somehow always did, call it grace.

Getting out of the car that day was like arriving by flying saucer on the planet earth still wrapped in its strangeness. Greg ignored keep out signs and investigated the facilities. He fell into conversation with a bloke who told him a lot in the short walk they took from car park to poolroom. In a mess hall he ate lasagna and salad after getting a meal ticket from a cook who welcomed him. There was a geologist, Eddie Slim, who came over with a smiling inquiry and less than an hour passed before Greg was in the wet canteen boozing.

It was the ideal job and Greg hadn't even known it was coming. On the phone he painted it to Jac as more or less local, home every weekend, but Pipeline Ranger was the designation and so Greg ranged indeed, wearing an Akubra under the blue sky and filling a bar-coded niche with his photograph laminated on plastic. Home again Jac laughed sideways, and said he looked bought up. Only one word was needed to renew their conflict and that was the one.

After the first time it was a month before he was back – Jac wondering about the charge the job gave his balls, same as if it had been another woman, she said, the corners of her mouth tensing. Sometimes he was poised within sight of the sea, other times found with red dust between his teeth on the farthest fling of the pipeline west. His boy and his girl loved the presents he brought them, Barbie dolls and GI Joes from old-time cluttered general stores, last minute grabbed.

Jackie incessantly asked what his feeling was, if only he could articulate the feeling he could do anything, go anywhere, make free with their lives she seemed to imply.

The word summarising it for Greg was waste, but how could he say that? Waste so intrinsically part of him it was beyond expression. She would think he meant his life was wasted with her, but no not that. Waste as defined by a process of nature, the wearing down of hills to the distant sea which he talked about with Eddie Slim as they sat in the purple dusk drinking themselves silly. Greg ached being part of it although hills didn't have feelings.

Of course an aeroplane was involved to overcome contradictions, a battered beauty sitting at the end of a dirt strip. A Maule taildragger, Greg ran his hands over her fuselage and wrestled mockingly with the prop as if he were enlivening a living depressive. When he took her up, snarling along ridges in late afternoon light, holding to steep low circles with g-forces dragging his cheeks, he knew he was ready to die. But didn't or wouldn't or couldn't.

The task was to talk into a mike interpreting and observing. Greg snarled the Maule over rocks and gullies in pursuit of its own dancing shadow a bare one hundred feet below. A spotter of broken fences, of scrub fires, of wild pigs and camels and horses, of tracked intrusions into a no-go zone. Greg was paid to think aloud, a connoisseur of himself. It was dollars for dreaming he declared on the quiet in case he spoiled his luck. Anyone who wanted to go for a spin he took them. Often it was Eddie Slim, that Trout Junction boy from the sixties who talked about going back, buying the piece of land he'd long had his eye on, except through successive well-heeled owners the price was truly hiked.

West of a dusty railhead there was a week when Jac came with the kids in the school holidays, the Honda loaded with camping gear. 'We apologise for our interruption,' she said, unable to make any utterance free from bitterness, taunt. They couldn't touch, or meet eyes really, yet had a treaty going when Greg flew, Jac settling something inside herself, alongside him, allowing her fate was all his for the skyborne duration.

It was gold-bearing country where mines opened in years when the Aus dollar meant profit; a country of quartzy ridges, scarred watercourses, cold winds over the saltbush plains. The gasfield itself was another five or six horizons north-west and Greg was thinking of nothing when a wink of mellow light came from a scraped arena during a lazy turn. He applied power and around he went again, noting the landmarks.

Over cold beers leaving olympic rings of condensation on a formica tabletop Eddie Slim told Greg how gas-bearing strata was mined. Down a borehole thousands of metres deep a gel mixed with tiny ball bearings was pumped under extreme pressure until a cap of rock was shattered and the gas released from that was taken off.

'Exciting stuff,' said Greg.

It was, said Slim, but not the same as gold, that mythical magma of the soul, and he gave Greg a smile that seemed to say he was on to him. But he couldn't possibly have been.

Next day Slim and Greg set off in Slim's Toyota for a scrub bash, taking Kim, Polly, and Marie, Eddie's fourteen-year-old, Greg asking them to keep their eyes peeled across claypans.

'For what?' asked Slim with that same amused sidelong glance he'd given last night.

Greg in his heart had a feeling of heavy excitement, a gambler's certainty. Astonishingly that same glint he'd seen from the air answered him on the flat. Implying no special reason for asking, Greg asked Slim to turn one-eighty degrees. The kids picked up on it although all Greg said was he saw a flash, as from broken glass.

'Gold?' Slim's Marie wondered. Greg hadn't mentioned gold. Not uttered the word once.

The vehicle stopped, the kids jumped out and started racing. It was in the papers, the legal wrangle, how ownership hung on mention of a word. Gold. For it had not been Greg Johnson who spoke it, but the geologist Eddie Slim and his precocious daughter – never Greg to whom gold must henceforth be described as having no earthly function or use, merely a product of time rolling its planetary weight over and excreting under pressure a mere essence of something unlived. In a word, waste.

Or so Jackie who pursued the Slims in court earned the right to think.

Slim's Marie reached the nugget, shouted her claim to Slim and squealingly attacked the soon to be celebrated lump, while the others watched, standing back as if from the heat of a blaze. Slim got around behind his girl and the pair wrenched it loose, quite unable to hold the prize, grasping its slippery lugs, clods of earth falling from pitted hollows of tremendous heaviness.

The nugget was called the Slim Find. It was displayed in Australia Square, an object of extravagant grandeur worth dollars in multiples of hundreds of thousands on the gold market, but to a pair of competing billionaires, bidding for the nugget intact, worth much more. Slim dealt with them, whatever it cost to his soul, and the Johnson claimants were awarded enough, after costs, for Jac's three-bedroom cottage mortgage-free after their separation. There she lived in Railway Street, Trout Junction. Greg kept the Honda. Whenever Greg called on Jac hoping for a bed for the night, nothing more, she found excuses and turned him away.

Reaching into his backpack Greg withdrew the bottle of single malt he'd carefully but self-deludingly stashed and refrained from telling himself he had the whole day long. How beautiful that spirit looked through its warps of glass when held to the last of light. A goblet, he called the small Pyrex tumbler he carried for the purpose of civilised enjoyment.

By the time he'd mixed his drink among the reeds the sky had done with day. Back on his tongue Greg tasted spiritous delight in the clarity of sand-filtered creekwater. A creek of stars flowed through night coldly descending to nose level, the sky bordered by high dark banks narrowed to the northwest, the direction Greg needed to go. He calculated two drinks would bring him to a point where striking up from the bank brought him onto the road. Rather than a blundering return through his own former paddocks he would then follow the road back to his car. The route would take him through the bottom of what used to be Tim Mitchell's land, a piece of clear going thanks to Mitchell's habit of stocking his paddocks on the principle of overkill. It was all Metro Water's now, but lessees kept packing in sheep per acre. Soon he would reach Claude Bonney's wetlands. On the creekbank horizon line the lights of Bonney's old house winked through the low frostiness as Greg navigated closer. People had it rented until the valley was flooded. Greg was almost to the end of his second drink, mentally juggling the idea of a third when a voice exploded from the creek ahead of him:

'Fuck! Fuckin' water! Fuckin' barbed wire!'

Greg cowered against the bank. Grunts and splashes came from a mere twenty metres away. As Greg wriggled to the top of the bank keeping a low profile a shot rang out and a plume of red gunfire sparked across the gully. Someone yelled: 'Anyone there?'

Lying prone, tasting gravel, heart thumping, Greg awaited the next shot. He could hear the raspy breathing of his fellow night-marauder crouched below in the reeds. Greg knew that whatever was happening was between two others and his presence in the night was excess to the drama.

But at that moment the ghost of himself detached from

his company without even the politeness of a farewell. Greg scrambled to his knees and headed off.

Later that night Greg appeared at Jackie's door, arguing his way in. God knows why she bothered, she said, but something about him made her reverse her previous stand – grass sticks in his hair, seedily drunk, that was expected, but a light that had always disturbed her was gone from his eyes. It wouldn't do to tell him that, that something was gone. He wouldn't know what to put in its place. It would kill him, trying.

CRAIG McGREGOR

Blood and the Nation

Craig was a guest at the Byron Bay Writers Festival in 1998, 2000, 2001, 2002 and 2003.

I

I rang Nathan from the Happy Holiday Inn at Surfers. Anything I could bring him back? 'Yeah,' he said, 'a couple of randy tarts.'

Randy tarts? Where do you get them from? And where does Nathan get a phrase like that from? I mean, say that at the WEA and you'd be up against the wall.

Nathan had broken up with his first wife. He had a girlfriend at Alice Springs and he was going to see her at Easter but he was living just south of the Queensland border and it seemed a hell of a long distance to carry a relationship over. Nathan was building his own house out of besser blocks, he had a budget of $25,000 for a complete house and he couldn't leave till he got the roof on, he explained. 'Otherwise I'll be cactus,' he said. I reckoned he'd be cactus if he left it till Easter to see his girlfriend but I didn't say anything. Nathan was a good builder. One of these days I might want him to build a house for me. Timber, maybe, instead of concrete blocks. He was going to bag the inside of the blocks because he was a good painter and bagger as well as carpenter, he'd learnt it when he was in Greece after the war. Maybe he was a good lover too. He had curly gold-grey hair which had once been beginner brown and crazy bright eyes and he smiled a lot. I mean, maybe there was nothing wrong with thinking of women as randy, maybe women did get randy, all the women's magazines said so, but it sort of offended the puritan in me to think women would go around trying to rip the pants off blokes they fancied in the front seats of cars, which was hard in these days of bucket seats, no wonder the back seats had become such a symbol in rock 'n' roll mythology. I'd always thought of getting randy and seduction as male prerogatives, though my daughter said that was just another sign of my irredeemable masculinism . . . But tart? Tart was unacceptable. You could have a jammy tart and a knave of tarts but calling a woman a tart or a bimbo or a nympho or an airhead was just another male exercise in one-upmanship, another dominance ploy by cock-and-ball obsessives who loved nothing better than finding some woman to perform sexual gymnastics with and then calling her a slut. At least I'd worked that one out. Without help from my daughter.

'Nathan, mate, you can't call 'em tarts,' I said.

'Listen, call 'em what you like,' said Nathan, laughing down the phone, 'but bring 'em home.'

'You got to pay for that in Surfers,' I said.

'I got a budget of twenty-five thousand dollars . . .' he began.

When I got back Nathan was working on the ute. Yet again. His friends had all gone surfing.

'The rear bearing's gone. Locked up. Had to hitch into town to get one from the wreckers. I was spewin',' he said from under the ute.

'Wouldn't they give you a lift?'

'Surf's up,' he said.

'Stuff it.'

'First southerly for a month. Big swell off the bay. That's why they live here,' he said.

'The non-working class,' I said.

'You oughta join the Nationals. They need a bloke like you.'

'Want a cup of tea?' I said.

'Did you bring back a meat pie?'

'You said *tarts*, Nathan.'

I heard him drop his spanner. 'You mean you didn't bring them as well?'

Over tea Nathan told me the story, again, of how he'd been working as a painter once with another bloke and they were hauling their heavy painting plank up the site wall by hand when the phone rang. 'Here, take this,' said Nathan, handing the bloke the pulley rope end. 'Be straight back.' When the call was over he got deflected by something; it was half an hour before he remembered the bloke with the rope. By this time his mate had just about both arms pulled out of his sockets; he was four storeys up the site wall, scared to let go, hanging on for dear life. 'He was cactus after that,' said Nathan. 'Couldn't pull the skin off a custard.'

That reminded Nathan of the time he saw a snake in the feed shed and grabbed it by the tail before he realised he didn't have room to swing it. It was a brown. It had just started to double back as Nathan headed for the door. 'Me hand was froze to it!' said Nathan. 'I knew me only chance was to get out into the open!' He made it through the door, past the tank stand and into the back paddock at a speed that Michael Johnson would have envied, trying to swing the snake above his head and hoping to Christ nothing was in the way. A brown is a brown. One bite and you're deadsville with the priest saying mass and your mates already into the fridge. If you swing it hard enough it can't double back and bite you. By the time he let the snake go his arm was bloody near broke, it ached like Tom the Tosser's. "Course, it served me right,' he said. 'I was tryin' to git the commune's eggs . . .'

Next week I went back to Surfers. It always gave me a charge seeing those old weather-stained shacks right next to the beach which had resisted the tide of development and now had the best spots on the coast. I didn't mind those enormous postmodern confections, all pink and blue and icing sugar, which gave the strip a sort of pastel *Miami Vice* look, and the pumped music over the PA system, and the waitresses who looked like tarts (?) and the tarts (?) who looked like film starlets (?) and the film starlets (?) who looked like Marina Mirage harlots (?), and the sunrise clouds turning Southport into Canaletto and the highrise shadows turning the sand sunless and the civic boardwalk turning the esplanade into Atlantic City, and I didn't even mind the turnoffs to the Isle of Capri and Fun City and Grumpy's Bar and the fabulous Happy Holiday Inn which happened to have the cheapest Discount Standby Budget O'Nite Rates on the strip, and though I had doubts about the Japanese shops owned by Japanese firms selling Japanese souvenirs to the Japanese tourists who thronged the main streets of Surfers, I didn't mind the Bathe Between the Flags signs in Arabic and the pandanus palms fenced off like exhibits and the concrete walkovers disgorging shoppers into the sand and the muscled health-gym men and women in pink Speedos and G-strings flaunting their follicles on the esplanade . . . but it was good to see the old stuff surviving.

'Mad buggers,' said Nathan. 'Should take the money and run. That's what they do round here.'

'Where?'

'Down the Bay. Where the lawyers live. Those fishin' blokes, they was only too pleased to piss off. Get out of the wind. And the sandflies. Buy a unit in town. Bit a luxury, mate. No more fuckin' fibro. That whole coast is gonna fall into the sea. So's Surfers.'

'They've built a seawall.'

'This coast, mate, this coast has been moving inland for a thousand years. Metre a year. Nothing can stop it.' He laughed. 'Ever been here in a cyclone?' He toppled his fingers onto the table, knuckles down. 'One by one. Into the sea.'

Every day jets followed the coastline north, ferrying tourists to the Gold Coast. Sometimes a helicopter. Sometimes a biplane. Sometimes an ultra-light. They skirted the hang-gliders and ospreys and brahminy kites hovering in the wind currents over the headland. Sometimes an Army chopper swooped down on the skinny-dippers and sunbakers in the green coves of the national forest. Well, it was better than the drug cops.

A week later we went for a surf at the main beach. The swell had gone. 'Always the way!' complained Nathan. '*Jesus, mate, ya shoulda been here yesterday, it woz PUMPIN', it woz GNARLY, it woz FILTHY, it woz BAD . . .*'

We got back into the ute and headed down the coast to Flat Rock. Past Deep Creek. Over the bridge at Main Arm. Past Shelly Beach. You couldn't call the names inventive but they told you what you wanted to know.

'Didn't they call one of these places after your family?'

'Yeah,' Nathan said briefly.

'Anyone left?'

'Nope.'

'How come?'

Nathan was desultorily looking for pippies in the low tide. Every now and then he stopped and swivelled in the wet sand, feeling for them with bare feet. All he'd found so far were a couple of oyster shells. 'Well, the white folks drove most of 'em away. In the bad old days. A few hung on round here. Shanties. Me own mum 'n' dad too. Lived in the bush just back of here.' He waved his arm. 'Then the gov'ment decided they needed to raise money so they held an auction.'

'Did your family go?'

Nathan laughed. 'They watched.' He was still swivelling for pippies. 'When it was over they had nowhere to live. Developers pulled the shacks down. Evicted 'em. One by one. Go to the reserve or go to hell.'

'Where'd you go?'

'The long paddock, mate! Four, five year. Never stopped travellin'. Up north, out to Alice. Got some work on the prawners. Worked at the Bight for a while, buildin'. Never stayed nowhere long.'

He had stripped off to the waist and I noticed again he had these long skinny legs and muscly barrel chest. No good for surfing. You needed to be a pocket rocket like Tom Carroll. But he knew how to scavenge a meal of pippies. Most of the time.

'Don't reckon there's any here,' I said.

'You wouldn't fuckin' know, mate.'

'At least I know a pippie from an oyster.'

'Oyster's got hair around it,' said Nathan, grinning. 'You gotta open it with your teeth.'

'That's a mussel,' I said.

'A muscle,' said Nathan patronisingly, 'is what the male of the species opens the oyster with.'

'What brought you back?' I said.

'Homesickness. Bloody homesickness. Y' wouldn't read about it. Lived up in the hills for a while, with the commune. Blackfellas was welcome there. Nowhere else.'

'It's still the bad days,' I said.

'Dunno. I got a house, mate, I'm a member of the bourgeoisie. Oh yeah, and we got our name on the best beach on the coast.' He stopped. 'But the mob can't live there no more.'

It seemed too simple. Too ruthless. Even for white men.

'But you had a farm there,' I said.

'Yeah,' said Nathan. 'For a while. Bananas. Crazy. Ever try to grow bananas by the sea?'

'They do at Coffs.'

'Not next to the beach. Not right up.'

'What happened?'

'It worked for a while. Me old man, he'd be up at daybreak, proppin' up with poles, sprayin', cuttin', choppin' back the weeds. Hard work. Too bloody hard. Only the Italians made a go of it.'

'I know. There's a place down south of Grafton called Little Italy.'

Nathan laughed. 'Little Boong-land, that's what they called our place.'

'One day they'll learn.'

'Anyways, it didn't last. Salt got into the plants. Ate 'em away. They turned brown before they turned ripe. Lost 'em all. I can still see it: the whole hillside, where the lawyers live. Turned brown.'

'Jesus.'

'One Christmas, my dad gave up. "Boys", he said, "we're leavin'".' Nathan held his arms out. 'It was this big, the eiderdown. We all slept under it. Dad, Mum, all the kids. The blanket brigade. Now, that *was* bad times.' He stopped. 'No fuckin' pippies here, mate. Let's give it away.'

A week later I managed to line some work up for Nathan and drove over to pick him up. His ute had broken down again. The house was coming on: he'd done all the footings and most of the plumbing and was now laboriously laying the concrete blocks. 'Hey, that's the fun part,' he said. 'You can see it risin' up every day like a piss-prick. Very satisfyin'.'

He was sleeping under a tarp in what he insisted on describing as the master bedroom; if it rained too hard he climbed into the ute. 'It's a better dosshouse than verricle,' he said. 'I reckon I might live here and drive the bloody shack around.'

Actually he wasn't a bad surfer. Rode an old malibu, reckoned it fell off the back of a truck; it was a bit like an ironing board, a real old plank, with a timber stringer down the centre and hardly any rocker in the nose and a chopped-off tail; 'that's where it fell off the truck.' It didn't have any fancy decals on it so Nathan reckoned he was going to design his own. He couldn't make up his mind between I'D RATHER BE IRONING or SNAP, with a big jagged break stencilled across the centre.

'You could paint it up like a bronze whaler,' I said helpfully.

'Fin's on the wrong side,' said Nathan. 'What about a zip fastener with this great banana stickin' out of it?'

'It's been done,' I said.

'I'm gonna do sumpin',' said Nathan. 'Directly.'

Directly meant any time in the next two years. In the meantime Nathan and I ferried our malibus down to the bay and charged through the short boards further in like King Neptunes, Nathan doing nose rides and me crouched down doing head dips. 'WATCH OUT, IT'S DOC SPOCK AND HIS FAITHFUL RETAINER!' yelled one of the boogie boarders. I tried to run him down. One less body to boogie . . .

'Not many Kooris into surfing,' I told Nathan.

'White fella's sport, boss,' he said in mock-pidgin.

'Started with the Hawaiians,' I said.

'Dem Hawaiians, dey pretty smart fellas,' said Nathan.

'You blackfellas pretty bloody smart too,' I said.

'We spend all the time singin', dancin', tellin' stories, fuckin' the black womens. No time for surfin', boss.'

'You call me boss one more time,' I said, 'and I'll knock your woolly head off.'

'Woolly,' said Nathan, 'is a very racist term.'

He was right, of course, about the tribespeople: they lived by the beach but they never developed a beach culture, it was more an estuary culture, that was where all the fish and oysters and crabs and shellfish were and that was where the middens grew, enormous levee-mound relics of the Bundjalung Nation as impressive in their way as the pyramids, but more domestic – there were no slaves in the Bundjalung Nation. It was a community of canoe people, and fishermen, and mud diggers, and hunters, and warriors: muscular bearded men with armbands and necklaces and an arsenal of throwing spears. Hunks. No time for surfing.

'One of these days,' I said, 'I'm going to write a history of the Bundjalung people.'

'That figures. Can't trust us mob to do it for ourselves.'

'Someone's gotta do it.'

'You write it,' said Nathan. 'I'm livin' it.'

One day it turned winter. I woke up and daybreak was a

pale seamless grey in the window. The sea had turned to slate and a westerly was whipping the tops off the waves in long disintegrating plumes like spray from a nozzle. For once there were no surfers. The wind had a real bite to it; I put on a jacket and found driftwood and mounds of cornflake weed washed up on the beach. Even the crabs had been driven underground.

Easter had long passed and Nathan still hadn't finished his house. I offered to give him a hand but he reckoned I was likely to chop it off with a chisel. Being sick had slowed him down. He said his girlfriend in Alice would understand but I wasn't so sure.

'Is it the girlfriend or the place?' I asked him.

'Ever been there?'

'No.'

'You got to go west of Uluru. Away from all the tourists and stuff. There's a lot of trees and scrub around Alice, it's like a garden. But out there in the desert, mate, there's nothin'. You can see the curve of the earth. It's like standin' on the beach and lookin' out across all that water and knowin' there ain't nothin' for thousands and thousands of kilometres. Pretty fuckin' scary. Scares me. But . . .' Nathan stopped . . . 'It's replenishment for the soul.'

'That's very New Age,' I said.

'You blokes ain't never gonna understand,' he said. 'You're covered in shit from arsehole to breakfasthole. Same with me. That's why I starve meself sometime. Get rid of it all.' He poked a finger in his hair. 'It's all up here, mate.'

I had to go to Surfers again and rang him, as before, on the job at the industrial estate, but nobody answered. I was away a week and when I got back his house was empty. It had the roof on but no doors or windows or floorboards; just the shell. The wind was blowing through it and in one corner I found an old mattress and some girlie magazines. No note. No message on the raw cement block. Nothing.

I hadn't known Nathan that long but I was a bit surprised. We'd been good surfing mates. And sometimes pub mates as well. I missed him.

The winter dragged on and it was another month before I suddenly remembered the ute. It was still there, behind the shack. Unlocked. It had a lot of rust around the door. The seat cover was split. In the glove box was a rusty oyster knife, some sweets wrappers, a Mitre 10 bargain sheet, and a rain-stained pencil scribble:

DON'T TRY TO FOLLOW ME. I AM GOING WHERE WHITE MAN'S MAGIC IS USELESS. TO THE NAVEL OF MY PEOPLE. ALSO TO FIND LORRAINE. YOU CAN HAVE THE UTE. IF YOUR LUCKEY I'LL BRING BACK SOME RANDY TARTS. KOORIS. HA HA.

He'd signed it *LOTHAR*.

Funny, we must have both been brought up on Mandrake. Gestures hypnotically. Slicked back hair, moustache, cape. Black-and-white art. Black/white. No fullbloods left. We're all half-bloods in the Nation.

II

The next time I saw Nathan was at The Channel. He had a tinnie with an old outboard on the back. There was a bit of a point break running and he was up to his knees in water, waiting for a gap between sets. 'What are you doing back here?' I shouted.

'Tryin' to catch some bloody fish,' he said.

'Where's your girlfriend?'

'Lorraine? Back in Alice.'

'How long you here for?'

Nathan shrugged. 'Dunno. Gotta finish the house. See you in the pub.'

The pub keeper had named one of his beers after the clan and the clan didn't like it. Especially as it was a brown ale. They said: how'd you like it if we named one of our home brews O'Reilly's Rotgut and flogged it in the main street? Now, maybe if you paid us a royalty . . . They had a few friendly and unfriendly arguments about it, which dragged on for months and threatened to develop into another Koori war, but finally the publican who wasn't a bad bloke and liked country-and-western and had a few other karmic points in his favour, like being an ex-AFL ruckman, agreed to call his beer Coast Bitter and Nathan and his mates went back to drinking in the public bar where they'd been hanging out ever since the whaling stopped.

'So how was the Alice?' I said over a schooner.

'Good 'n' bad. Lorraine was good, the town was bad. Rednecks. They pave the streets with 'em over there. Couldn't wait to get out.'

'Did you go up country?'

'Yeah, real desert stuff. Out past Papunya, Utopia . . . Utopia!' He dragged a hand across his mouth. 'Them whitefellas, they got a sense of humour.'

'Good art.'

Nathan gave me one of his 'we-belong-to-different-cultures-and-you-ain't-ever-gonna-fuckin'-understand' looks. 'Out of the bottom of a petrol can.'

'The blues,' I said. 'The blues came out of dispossession.

And forged a symbol of alienation for the whole human race. There's got to be some pluses. From the history, I mean. From the history of the nation.'

'See ya later,' Nathan said.

It rained all that week. Up the hill it felt like being in Noah's ark. The swell came wrapping around the point in sheet metal arcs and toppled over in walls which streamed gigantic white veils behind them like Arthur Boyd's bride and closed out all the main beaches; even the malibus wouldn't go out. There were kestrels high off the cape and gannets diving through the salt spray and a lone bedraggled kurrawong which stumbled onto the verandah, swallowed some bits of bread, and flew off again. The land was so waterlogged it squelched every time you went outside. The fish shops stopped selling fish because the trawlers couldn't get out. Nor anyone else. Made you realise why the rainforest ran right down to the coast.

I found Nathan in the pub, drinking alone.

'Bad weather for fish.'

'And fishermen,' he said. 'Just my luck. Haven't been able to get the tinnie out for a week. Got any work on?'

'There's always my extra bedroom.'

'Too bloody hard, china. Anythin' else?'

'The sleepout. It needs some louvres.'

'Glass?'

'Timber,' I said. 'I'm trying to keep this weather out. Faces west, wrong side altogether. You'd have to frame it up, measure up the louvres, get 'em made somewhere . . .'

'I'm your man, boss.'

'I told you about that, Nathan.'

Nathan gave me one of his big Satchmo-Uncle Tom smiles. 'Just testin'.'

He was a good worker. He'd dump his trannie on the

floor next to his battered leather tool bag, tune it into the local FM, set up his sawhorse and drop sheet, and graft away for hour after hour. And sometimes he'd explain to me about the nation.

'Used to have hundreds of diffrent languages,' he said. 'Every mob, diffrent language. Most of them gone now. A few of the old people, they hang onto 'em, try to teach the young 'uns but they don't want to know, they're more interested in grog and footie and girls . . .'

'And boys,' I said.

'Makes no difference, because we all got the common language now.'

'What's that?'

'English. Abo English. Not pidgin, mind you. Real Abo English. Y'see, after the invasion, after so many of the peoples got killed, they put all those who were left in these big camps, groups from all over the place, who couldn't speak to each other, couldn't understand nothin', so they had to speak English. But they used a lot of the old words as well, pickin' 'em up from the different nations, see, and some of 'em were much the same anyways, like koori and murri, and after a while we got our own language – like it ain't just words, it's the way you say 'em, so the white folks wouldn't understand. Or if they did, they'd have to try a bit harder, see.'

'Keeps the coloniser on the back foot.'

'It woz, kind of, resistance. Surviving at all was resistance.'

'And now?'

'Now we can speak to one another. We got a common language for the first time, like we got a common cause. Alright. The white fella, and the watjiin, they got to watch out for the clever fella now. They got to pay the rent.'

'What's some of the words?'

'Aw . . . I dunno, gubba don't need to know. We speak it when the mob gits together for sorry business. Other business too. Speak the same way, most times. That way we keep our peoples alive.'

Nathan took a breather from his sawing, wiped his face with his flannelette shirt.

'Don't have to be a burnt potato.'

It hung in the air. Nathan went back to his sawing. Finally I couldn't resist.

'What's a burnt potato?'

'Coconut. Burnt potato. Black on the outside, white inside.' Nathan grinned. 'I knew you'd want to know.'

'Ain't any burnt potatoes around here,' I said.

'No,' said Nathan. 'Only fuckin' colonisers. Here, can y' give us a hand?'

That night, standing in front of the mirror, I tried to concoct a list of signifiers for the students. Striptease semiotics. *Bush hat:* Symbol of rural upbringing. *Moustache:* Signifies artist/maleness/hip-to-the-hip-without-being-hip. *Black coat:* Authority. *Flannel shirt:* Westie education. *Wedding ring:* Conventional bourgeois morality. *Eternity ring:* Uxuriousness/even more conventional bourgeois morality. *Corduroys:* Academic. *Blue singlet:* Allegiance to working-class culture. *Silver neckchain:* Peacock Oztralian. *Swatch:* Exquisite good taste masquerading as self-denial. *Jockey underpants:* Old age. *Vasectomy scar:* Ambivalent signifier: denotes lust/end of lust. *Black-and-ochre wristband*: allegiance to Aboriginal struggle/white appropriation of black resistance?

The problem ran right through our culture.

Even naked, I am Baudelaire's forest of symbols.

Two days after the storm abated a swell was still wrapping

around the point: fat slow waves with a drop like a lift shaft and a short glide to the right. I dragged out the kneeboard and found it was easier surfing in than paddling out; the shore break was perpendicular and the only way around it was to launch off from the rocks below the cape. With fins this was a problem. Without fins it was even more of a problem: getting sucked back onto the rocks is like being shredded on a grater. I opted for the fins, waited a long time for a break between sets, paddled out till my breath hurt.

Nathan was there. With his mates.

'Never thought you'd make it!'

I lay prone on the kneeboard and tried to think of an answer.

'Rescue me, darling,' I said.

His mates looked at Nathan. Nathan looked at me. I looked at the decal on the nose: BAY AREA SPOON.

'Last time I buy you a schooner,' he said.

'I'm waiting for the first.'

The next set loomed up and the mob disappeared. I paddled out towards the point so I wouldn't be caught inside. It can be lonely there. Oily waves. Seagulls. Maybe pelagic fish. Sharks . . .

The sun had transformed the bay into glittering metallic silver, mercury-shine, black rocks silhouetted like shadows against fireburst. I waited for a smaller wave, took the drop, sliced through the white water, overturned, got washed up on the sand. On my back. With fins you're as clumsy as a marooned sealion.

'Very graceful,' said Nathan, who was watching. 'Very delicate. Absolute control.'

His mates were gone.

'I promise never to call you darling again,' I said.

'Better not. I'd be cactus.'

When the sleepout was finished Nathan decided to get to work on his own house again. The ute was still buggered so I would take him out to the building site in the morning and pick him up again in the afternoon. He was staying with some of his kinship mob in town who he reckoned owed him one anyhow. Some of them worked, some of them surfed, most of them drank and hung around. 'No work in this shithole,' said Nathan. 'Half the town's on welfare. Kooris are worst off. Last to get a job, first to get laid off.'

'Then why stay here?'

'This is our stake,' Nathan said. 'The nation started here. It's gonna end here too. No bullshit. We ain't gonna be driven out.'

'Lorraine?'

'Out past Alice, that's our place too. But it's diffrent, see. Diffrent mob. Diffrent place. Down there where the middens are, my family used to feast down there. I remember that, from when I was a kid. We named this place. We *made* it. One of these days we gonna take it back. Directly.'

'You're going to need help.'

'Maybe. Maybe not. You get help, the helpers take you over. I've read my black history.'

'So have I,' I said. 'When Afro-Americans turned against the Jews they lost their best allies. Black racism. You can't justify it.'

'I woz talking about *here*. Blokes like you,' said Nathan. 'Anyways, maybe Lorraine'll come here.'

It kept raining. Work on the house was slow. Sometimes a week would go by and nothing would happen. Building a house by yourself is one of the hardest things a man can do. As Lillian Roxon used to say, it pays to install helpers.

Repeat after me: to help is to incorporate. To incorporate is to subsume. After the subsumption, the Colony reinstates. Itself.

When he got the gal iron roof over one room, Nathan disappeared. Same story. Empty house, empty ute. Not even a note this time. He's left his tool bag in my car, so I assumed he'd be back. But the months went on, and the season turned over. The tourists faded like a bad memory, and the pub put coal braziers out in the courtyard, and the only people in the main street were surfers with woollen beanies pulled down over their ears.

I thought of writing, but as usual I had no address, and something stopped me going around to his community's house.

I had a four-wheel-drive, and they didn't.

I suppose I could have walked.

Anyway, with the cold current still running off the coast, and whale watchers up near the lighthouse, and only a few shivering Malibu riders in wetsuits keeping the faith, I started avoiding the pub and settled for hot chocolates at the alternative café near the post office.

Cold mid-morning. Scanning the latest massage and spiritual healing and tarot reading flyers in the window, I noticed a familiar figure stroll past. With a woman. Curly gold-grey hair, slender arms, casual gait. That was Nathan. The woman was white.

'G'day,' I said.

'G'day,' said Nathan.

'Long time no see.'

'Went back to the Alice, told ya I would.'

'You could've left a note.'

'Too sentimental. This is Lorraine.'

'Pleased to meet you,' she said.

'Same here,' I said. She was in her forties, dumpy, straight brown hair, real friendly smile. 'I've heard a lot about you, but . . .'

Nathan grinned at me. 'I never told you she was white, did I?'

'No.'

'One of these days, me china, you're gonna stop thinkin' of me as black,' he said, 'and then you'll be free.'

DI MORRISSEY
Talking Up a Festival

Di has been a Byron Bay Writers Festival supporter and a guest since 1998 and has appeared at eight Festivals.

The downside to being a writer is – you have to know how to talk.

It's not enough to write a book – you have to get out there and pump it up, through the media, promotional appearances, lunches, dinners, library teas, writers festivals, and to, well, anyone who'll listen really.

Some writers flourish in the limelight and are terrific at Speaking. Some writers love to be centre stage but are dreadful spruikers for their work, some get sweaty palms and palpitations at the mere thought.

They come out at writers festivals. On panels, on stage, in conversation, signing books, swanning, pitching a new book, hustling agents, publishers and publicists. Or hiding in the wings, behind a tent, or in the bar.

You've arrived as a writer when you're invited to participate in a festival.

In my case it took some time. Festivals used to take themselves frightfully seriously. Writing is a serious business apparently, and the literary establishment did not take lightly to writers who were popular, sold books and appeared on TV too much. Among the *serious* writers there seemed an undercurrent of world-weary angst, everything being a struggle, from wrangling the muse to rounding up those words and corralling them on the blank page, to being misunderstood and unappreciated by agents, the media, editors, publishers. Cripes, give me a break. Why do it? I asked. Where's the fun?

I was quite happy to have published six best-selling books and not been invited to any festival or function that smacked of acceptance into the world of elite REAL writers. (And if you're feeling neglected and unappreciated as a writer, take my dear friend Robert Dessaix who is a Real Writer of exquisite prose and thoughtful and funny to boot. In all the years he has been writing, broadcasting and publishing he only just received his first ever award. Accolades galore but never a tangible prize. In this instance, the Victorian Premier's Prize. When he admitted being thrilled to receive his gong, as it was his first ever, an audible gasp went round the room. Everyone assumed he'd had plenty.)

Then I wrote *The Songmaster*, which grew from my experience of staying with Aboriginal people in the Kimberley and becoming involved in the then unknown concept that came to be known as Reconciliation.

So I was invited to the Melbourne Writers Festival.

Knowing my publisher had put my name forward several times before and been knocked back, I had no great inclination to accept. Anyway, I was scared stiff at the idea. It had been made very clear to me that popular fiction (read: lightweight, frivolous, shallow) authors did not get invited to writers festivals.

Like I didn't actually *write* my books, as in crafting words in sentences. They somehow got sprayed on the page like hair lacquer or perfume. And the idea that I might redraft, rewrite and care about what I wrote was not considered. And because I published a book a year, I was referred to as 'churning them out'. Tossing them off like flipping a pancake.

Never mind I had No Life for most of the year.

In my first nine years as a published author I was able to establish myself, spend time researching, then lock myself away in singular and solitary confinement while I wrote. I was able to do this because I was alone. No partner, kids away at university in America and only home during vacation (when they were kept occupied at the beach and with friends), my family safely down in Sydney. I spent six to eight hours a day writing, seven days a week. That's how I wrote a book a year. But I wasn't going to say that.

However, my publisher and head of publicity gently coaxed me round. It was an *honour* to be invited to a prestigious festival. Of course people will know who you are. Of course people will be nice to you. Of course people will come to hear you. Of course it will raise your profile with the media (who do not take me seriously as I'm blonde, been on TV and, worst of all, been successful). Oh, really?

I was petrified. I'd never been to a writers event of any kind. I had no idea what went on, how authors conducted themselves. How did one interact with them? With the audience? I was told I'd appear on a panel discussing a subject themed vaguely to some connection with my work. I jumped up and down pleading I not be associated in any way with romance writing. That's not what I write but was constantly presented as one who did. Very little likelihood of *that*, I was told – this is a *writers* festival. Phew.

So I went, and found myself surrounded by ladies whom I *could* describe as terrifying left-wing feminists, but I won't. They were excruciatingly articulate and oozed a self-righteous confidence that was meant to, and did, intimidate me. And I also realised I was dressed inappropriately. I wore colours. And jewellery. And pink lipstick. I quickly observed that some of the other writers who read their work well, and knew it, had perfected speaking and reading aloud to the degree that it became Performance.

I was not in any comfort zone. Behind the podium my knees were shaking so badly one leg threatened to collapse. I read my prepared piece, avoided eye contact – not that I could see as the lights were bright – and sat down as the next speaker spoke without notes way beyond our allotted time. We were then ushered out to sign books in a throng of crushing bodies in an old building that I cannot recall clearly except I hated being there. I believe I was hyperventilating. One dear old lady wanted to talk to me as I signed her book, but she was moved smartly along, as were we panelists, as the next session was starting.

I had a second event and held onto my publicist's hand, shaking with terror, to be led into the slaughterhouse once more. Oh God, this time the chairs were lined up in the centre facing the audience seated in ringed tiers that disappeared into dark reaches of the theatre's gantry. The subject had something to do with white approaches to Indigenous culture or something. I think I was the only woman on the panel. After I had been ignored by everyone on my previous panel, when one fellow leaned over and said something chatty I nearly put my head in his lap and wept.

I was warned that no one would have actually read any of my books, but I'd have loyal readers 'out there'. There were no gladiators in this arena. There was no podium or microphone to hide behind either. We sat in a row, exposed, shuffling papers on our laps. And so one by one we delivered our earnest, and I believe passionate and well-intentioned, pieces. The audience clapped. And the Chair called for questions. There was silence. Followed by silence. I glanced at the erudite friendly man beside me. He shrugged. So I spoke up and suggested I ask the audience a question. Which I did. And which someone answered and we were thankfully away and got into a stimulating debate.

In a post-mortem with my team from the publishers I was told I'd done well. Just a few little things, like – you never mention another author in your talk, let alone praise them. Unless they're dead. And maybe it'd be a good idea to do what some of the others did and talk up how good you are at what you do and how well you sell and how people just get lost in your books that challenge and stimulate them.

It's called selling yourself, Di.

Are you joking? I can't do that.

In my days as a TV presenter I interviewed a lot of actors. (Writers were not welcome on TV in those days as they were considered boring talking heads.) I thought actors were neurotic, ego-driven, incestuous talkaholics – until I started to mix with authors!

So I avoided festivals, apart from the Byron Writers Festival where I felt at home. But then I was invited to the Adelaide Festival Writers Week.

The publishers didn't have to convince me that this was an honour, and, they reckoned, I'd be the first popular fiction author to present. I was wobbly-kneed again looking at the other guests, from Isabel Allende, Margaret Atwood, JM Coetze, Etgar Keret from Israel, local stars like Kate Grenville, Graeme Blundell . . . oh, the list was staggering.

It was hot, non-stop work, from doing media to squeezing into other authors' talks and panels, attending Aussie publishers', overseas agents' and international publishers' parties. We all stayed at the one hotel and the late-night bar was a continuous party.

Prior to Adelaide I'd been on a huge book tour talking at three events a day in a different town a day, and was losing my voice. But I was thrilled to be there.

I kept nudging Jane, my publicist. 'Guess what Isabel said to me at breakfast.' I had a handbag full of name-dropping anecdotes. I really thought I'd arrived when I walked back into the lobby of the Hilton to find Margaret Atwood walking towards me, arm outstretched, pointing.

'My dear . . . *where* did you get that hat?'

So I told her and we talked about the trials of hat packing on the road and I promised to send her one. In black. Which I did. My white one is now known as the Margaret Atwood Hat. So Adelaide was a small triumph, and more – I enjoyed myself.

When I was invited to the inaugural Writers Festival on Norfolk Island I figured I could get into this. I mean, it included a partner, it was for a week with a not too onerous schedule, time was allotted for water activities, my old friend Sorrell Wilby was living there, and the fishing sounded beaut. Too bad it was winter.

It was my first time on the island. It was after the Patton murder and no suspects had been turned up, but rumours were murmured behind hands.

Whether it was the grey wet sky, the wind that cowered the pines, the churning sea or the cloud hanging over the unsolved murder, we felt to be in the middle of a gothic movie.

We were billeted in holiday accommodation around the

island. Our cottage faced a steep green hillside where the sea hit the rocks. Parting the curtains on the first morning was like viewing the stage set for a creepy play. Bad vibes abounded, declared my partner, who felt justified when we were told The Body had been found in front, 'just down there on that plinth'.

There was a bonding among the writers, an eclectic group with a lot of nonfiction authors from other walks of life, like Richard Morecroft, Doris Brett, Richard Zaccharia, Marie Mahood, and authors who'd sold millions like Bradley Trevor Grieve. There was the inevitable 'loner' who kept to himself, the unruly Bob Barrett. But it was an interesting group and we soon had the town sussed, persuading a restaurant to stay open late so we could adjourn for supper after the last evening session, and it would be worth their while to keep the bar open as well.

As there was only one venue, we all tried to attend each other's sessions, but understood if there was a scuba, fishing or shopping expedition to distract instead.

It was well attended by visitors from the mainland, and after the opening address by patron Colleen McCullough – who spoke at astonishing length – we felt very much a family. Maybe it was because we were on an island that we bonded. We befriended locals and all got different theories on the murder. Several of us planned books, of course.

I was one of the first to speak. I put my notes aside and spoke from the heart about my life. I was teased a bit, but it gave others the freedom to toss out prepared talks and thus open the confessional floodgates. We all had a splendid week.

I moved to Byron Bay sixteen years before the sea changers, but then more 'creatives' started to drift into my home town. Creative types who'd actually worked professionally as opposed to all the navel-gazers sitting on one latte in the Byronian talking about the book that's in their heads, or busy saluting the sun at Belongil.

And so a small group started to mutter about our own festival. It grew organically as things do in Byron, from an idea mooted in the post office or Woolies, to a larger group in someone's living room. From a sputtering start, she took off.

Part of Byron's success has been the venue, a modest older resort (known as the Gulag by those more at home in five-stars) with cabins scattered in lush gardens, a lake, a golf course and a track to the beach. Session venues are big tents, a small conference centre by the lake, the dining room and verandah. So everyone lives, works, speaks, plays and parties at the same site.

It has been the scene of many skirmishes as well. From robust debate between authors and free-wheeling Byronites, to great ideas expressed and exchanged, to baggy-eyed breakfast gossip.

Each festival has its own scandal. The couple making out on the beach was not an unusual sight perhaps, but *she* is a star author and *he* is a rival publisher. And what about the shambling, unkempt Big Name Writer who was hitting on any female within radius as if he was George Clooney. Through an alcoholic haze he stumbled into a young woman and asked if she'd like a fuck. Her riposte was she'd love one – but not with him. Call her picky, but did she visualise doughy white flesh, spraying dandruff, odorous breath and questionably clean undergarments?

And then again there was the Famous Writer, a known recluse, lured to Byron by its laid-back ambiance, good surf and the promise of a private residence. He didn't expect to be put up at a plush resort. Or carted to the Festival in a white limo.

The Famous Writer would have been much happier doing his own thing. I offered him my old spare station wagon that'd fit his surfboard in, but I was informed he was far too famous to drive himself. (Famous writer would have choked knowing that.)

Early on, after my own festival experiences, I thought it would be nice to invite the visiting writers, a publisher or two and others to my house for drinks as a bit of a kick-off before being thrown together publicly.

Di's Drinks was an instant hit. Why not – free booze and food, a chance to wander through the fairy-lit tropical garden, hang out in my house and actually have conversations at length with interesting people in the same field that one has never met before. Byron is a friendly place, laid-back, warm in spirit as well as climate, and where freedom of speech – even the maddest of utterings – is tolerated.

It became a tradition. It became a legend. It became a nightmare, growing as the Festival grew. There was no way we could limit invitations. But as the party, co-hosted now with my publisher, Pan Macmillan, became bigger and an expected event, so it became less fun for me. And the house was never meant to entertain 200 people. By the time the lawn had recovered, we'd fished the last chicken bone out of the bushes away from the dog, the repairs to the Oriental carpets had been made, and the stories squashed, it was time for next year's party.

Looking back over the highlights, it was not the agent falling into the rose bushes, the heated political arguments, the ignition of love affairs, or the marginally known author who, in her cups, ear-bashed two commissioning publishers who had not a clue who she was or what she'd written, until it registered they weren't au fait with her work – or cared – and the author lost it, beating her chest and screaming, 'Just google me!'

It was the extraordinary array of guests that made it special, from former prime ministers to a president, to a major movie star, to authors I knew only by name and what they'd written and then discovered they were the most wonderful people (Li Cunxin comes to mind), and the friendships which continue.

Byron is a festival that caters to the punters, the readers who buy our books. Wandering around the Festival gardens, sitting on the lawn, under an umbrella at a table with a locally grown coffee, readers and authors can exchange views informally. And reader feedback is not to be ignored.

Ideas blossom, conversations are enjoyed, we all get to hear views, funny anecdotes, passionate forums that lift us above the contrived, the manipulated and the humdrum.

This is what makes Byron special. Maintaining our uniqueness will be the challenge of the future.

THEA ASTLEY
Why I Wrote a Short Story Called 'Diesel Epiphany'

Thea was a guest at the Byron Bay Writers Festival in 2003 and in 2004, which was her last public appearance before her death in August 2004.

I should explain, I suppose, that I'm not a very accomplished traveller. Some people are expert at it, but things, awful things, seem to happen whenever I board a plane train bus. Actually, I don't do too much plane boarding because I can never afford to travel more than cattle class. This is the sort of thing that happens when I leave the safe perimeters of my patch: once when I was staying in the Marlborough Sounds and had gone driving with friends in the afternoon, I came back to my motel room at four o'clock and the Ambassador for Lebanon was asleep in my bed. Now I didn't think for a minute that he was one of those courtesy presents they sometimes give you in hotels, like the shower cap and the two pieces of fruit and the mending kit. It wasn't a hotel like that. So I went down to the office and I said there's a very large dark man – and I'm almost sure he's foreign – asleep in my bed and they said oh that is the Ambassador for Lebanon. We have changed your room. And then they moved me to a kind of spare room they used for the gardener.

And the year before that there was the moose. Somewhere between Calgary and Regina our Greyhound bus hit a moose. There we were at two in the morning shuddering in the autumn cold of the prairie, caught up for an hour while the driver inspected damage to his headlights and waited for the west coast bus to come through. Anyway, after this hour of half-doze the lights suddenly snapped on and the driver went right down the bus handing out questionnaires for us to fill in: nature of accident; estimated speed of bus; estimated speed of moose; nationality (of moose?), sex, purpose of travel, visit. Signature. Can moose write? There was one of those hissed domestics going on in the seat in front of us. The husband kept saying, Will you forget the goddam moose. The moose is just fine. Why don't you worry about the goddam bus, for Chrissake. You're riding in the bus, aren't you? You're not riding the goddam moose.

The seat in front of us was full of snivels and as if this wasn't enough we're an hour late into Regina and four passengers crawl in from the bus shelter and there are only three seats and the driver says, Will that woman who got on with her husband mind getting off, and the woman, who was big and black, says, I ain't got no husban. Ah'd like a husban. And this snaps the bus wide awake and a voice cries from down the aisle, You get her a husban. And there's a general cackle and then the whole bus starts calling, Don't you get off till he finds you a husban, and I hear the woman in front of me say, She can have mine, and then this couple sulk all the way to Chicago. I mean you can FEEL their sulks.

I think buses are worse in Australia. Or maybe it's the drivers. There are those bus captains who seem to be training to be sit-down comics. They have a mike and a PR system and it's like the breakfast show all night or they play country and western and metal rock or conduct community singing. They crack funnies. There was one driver on the southern run who used to say at comfort stations, Now don't forget the number of the bus. Write it on the back of the person in front and don't let them out of your sight. I remember a party of lady bowlers who sang hearty songs with risqué choruses non-stop from Gladstone to Brisbane. And another time on the Gold Coast run a young man behind me (what was it Bob Ellis said about the beauty of the monologue?) told his life story loudly to an uninterested grunting passenger. By Surfers he'd covered his life to eighteen, his father's life to fifty, his first six jobs, his father's one job. By Grafton he'd gone thoroughly into four girlfriends and was metaphysically examining the failure of the relationship with his fifth when this gentle little man across the aisle from me swung round and snarled, Forget her, son, and let me forget her too. I can't stand it, he said. I can't stand it another minute. I'll kill him. I'll kill the driver. I'm seventy-one and I don't have to stand it. The last time I went to the Centre I told the driver either you lower that music or you put me off and I'll walk. Right here in the middle of nowhere. And I started to tug at the door and I said, You ought to be ashamed. When the newspapers get hold of this it won't look too good, an old bloke of seventy put out to walk from Oodnadatta. So then he lowered the godawful music. And then the old man gave up trying to sleep and he told me he had this fantasy about buses that did the Wagner run and the Brahms run or something, and he liked to think of all the passengers getting excited when the driver said, Now folks, can we have a bit of hush?

I'm putting on the Elgar second, and all the Norms and Berts get all worked up and say, Shut up, love, it's the Elgar second. Then he stopped talking suddenly and began to wrestle with his ear plugs. I'd like to think he got his dream but maybe he had to ask to be put off. I'll never know, because we got off at Macksville at four in the morning and then the horror began from a different angle. We'll leave the key to your room on the table near the office, the hotel had assured us on the phone. There was no key. Maybe they've left it in the door, I suggested. Country pubs do that. So we went upstairs and Jack went down one corridor while I went down another and I found a door with a key in it and I opened the door and felt for the light switch in one efficient movement and the naked bulb blazed down and there was this terrible moaning from the bed and I said, Oh God, I'm so sorry, and shut the door smartly and then realised I'd left the light on so I unlocked the door again and the man in the bed let out a sharp cry that cut right through my apologies so I took my humiliation away to the smoking room and lay on the floor with my head on my overnight bag and after a while, a long while, Jack came back and he said, Hey, there was one door with a key in it. I guess you heard him shouting.

I really don't want to think about buses. Trains have the personality, the tension, the romance of all travel – of waiting-rooms and tea-rooms and the music of the rackety lurch. And with luck you can sleep on trains. And here's another once. First class this time somewhere between Augsburg and Nuremburg and Germany is in darkness though there are lights across the swept fields and the pruned hedgerows. I have the compartment to myself, my bag's on the rack, my shoes off, and I'm hoping for sleep all the way to Hamburg. But just then one of the attendants comes in to check my ticket and he's an elderly frayed man and despite the pressed affirmations of his uniform he looks tired as if perhaps he has done this run too long. He has little English and I have no German except Lieder titles, but in a major effort to communicate, as we pass through Nuremburg without stopping, I point out a fierce blaze of townlight and neon. Die Meistersinger, I say. His whole body seems to awake as if a finger has prodded nerve spots of his nostalgia.

Opera, he asks. You like?

I shake my head and say Lieder. Lieder. I like Lieder. Dietrich Fischer . . .

Dieskau, I say hopefully. And then to my surprise he smiles fully, widely and leans forward.

Gerhard Husch, he says. Ah.

Elisabeth Schwarzkopf, I offer. It's like a competition.

Hans Hotter, he says.

Irmgaard Seefried, I say.

Anneliese Rothenberger, he says. And I laugh.

In Australia, I manage with difficulty, train conductors don't know Anneliese Rothenberger.

Ah, he says. They know the Beatles?

We are filled with mutual delight.

On and on the train goes. On and on we go, offering singers' names to each other like small bouquets of respect.

Wilhelm Strienz.

Lotte Lehmann.

Christa Ludwig.

Gottlob Frick.

I remember the old man on the bus. Ah, I think in my turn. Ah.

CONTRIBUTORS

Thea Astley (1925–2004) was born in Brisbane and studied at the University of Queensland. First published in 1958, she was the author of sixteen books. Her first collection of short stories, *Hunting the Wild Pineapple*, won the Townsville Literary Foundation Award in 1979, and *It's Raining in Mango* won the Steele Rudd Award and the 1988 FAW ANA Literature Award. *A Kindness Cup* won the *Age* Book of the Year Award in 1975, *Beachmasters* won the Australian Literary Society Gold Medal in 1987, and *Reaching Tin River* won the New South Wales Premier's Award for fiction in 1990. She was the recipient of the Patrick White award in 1989. *The Multiple Effects of Rainshadow* won the *Age* Book of the Year in 1996. She won the Miles Franklin Award four times: in 1962 for *The Well Dressed Explorer*, in 1965 for *The Slow Natives*, in 1972 for *The Acolyte* and in 2000 for her last novel, *Drylands*. Thea moved to the Byron Bay area in 2003 where she spent the last two years of her life.

Jean Bedford is a novelist and short-story writer who has published ten books of fiction and edited several others, both fiction and non-fiction. She has been a journalist, a publisher's editor and a teacher, most recently of creative writing. She was a member of the Byron Bay Writers Centre Committee for several years and a regular contributor to the Byron Bay Writers Festival. She lives with her husband, Peter

Corris, on the Illawarra coast near Wollongong and lectures in Writing at UTS.

Alison Broinowski, a former Australian diplomat, has written or edited nine books on aspects of the interface between Australia and Asia. She is a member of the Australian Republican Movement, the Asian Studies Association, the Paddington Society, and a Council member of Sydney PEN International and the Australian Institute of International Affairs (NSW). Her best known books are *The Yellow Lady: Australian Impressions of Asia* (OUP, 1992 and 1996) and *About Face: Asian Accounts of Australia* (Scribe, 2003). Her latest book, co-written with James Wilkinson, is *The Third Try: Can the UN Work?* (Scribe Publications, 2005).

Susan Bradley Smith lectures in Writing at Southern Cross University. Widely published as a theatre historian, most recently co-editing *Playing Australia: Australian Theatre on the World Stage*, she is currently researching in the area of creative writing and the medical humanities. *Griefbox and Other Plays* was published in 2001, and a collection of poetry, *Tractor*, is forthcoming with Salt. Her memoir, *Friday Forever*, will be published by Radcliffe in 2006.

Larry Buttrose is a novelist, travel writer and journalist. His most recent books are the novel *Sweet Sentence*, and the nonfiction work *People Who Have Changed the Modern World: From Einstein to Eminem*.

John Carroll is Professor of Sociology at La Trobe University in Melbourne. He has degrees in mathematics, economics and sociology from the universities of Melbourne and Cambridge. His recent books include *Ego and Soul: The Modern West in Search of Meaning* (1998), *The Western Dreaming* (2001), *Terror: A Meditation on the Meaning of September 11* (2002) and *The Wreck of Western Culture: Humanism Revisited* (2004).

He has edited *Intruders in the Bush: The Australian Quest for Identity* (1982, 1992) and, together with Robert Manne, *Shutdown: The Failure of Economic Rationalism* (1992). He is also a frequent writer of essays and newspaper articles, and delivered one of the *Alfred Deakin Federation Lectures* in 2001. His work focuses on modern Western society, and in particular on the forces that alternatively hold it together and press towards disintegration. He chaired the panel reviewing the National Museum of Australia in 2003.

Peter Corris's first novel was published in 1980, and he has been a full-time writer since 1982. He is credited with reviving the fully fledged Australian crime novel, with local settings and reference points, and with a series character firmly located in Australian culture (Cliff Hardy). Peter Corris hopes that his latest non-crime book, *The Journal of Fletcher Christian*, will underline his credentials as an historical novelist. This thoroughly researched book circles back to his earlier career as a Pacific historian and journalist, but, as Corris says, 'There is no better training for a novelist than history and journalism.' He lives on the Illawara coast of New South Wales with his wife, writer Jean Bedford, and their three daughters.

Nick Earls is the author of eleven books, including bestsellers such as *Zigzag Street*, *Bachelor Kisses* and *Perfect Skin*. Four of his novels have been adapted successfully into plays by La Boite, and *48 Shades of Brown* has been adapted into a feature film. He appeared at the Byron Bay Writers Festival with the release of *48 Shades of Brown* in 1999, *The Thompson Gunner* in 2004 and in 2006 with his latest novel, *Monica Bloom*.

Peter Goldsworthy's most recent book is *The List of All Answers: Collected Stories* (Penguin). He has won literary awards in the genres of poetry, the short story and the novel, and a Helpmann Award, together with

Richard Mills, for the opera *Batavia*. His first play, an adaptation of his 1992 novel *Honk If You Are Jesus*, premiered at the 2006 Adelaide Festival to considerable critical acclaim.

Kate Grenville has written seven works of fiction and three 'how-to-write' books (one in collaboration with Sue Woolfe). Her latest novel, *The Secret River*, based on her own family history, is the story of an ex-convict settler and his relationship with the Aboriginal people. It has been a bestseller since publication and won the regional Commonwealth Writers' Prize for 2006 and the Fellowship of Australian Writers Award, as well as being published in the United Kingdom, the United States and Canada and in translation. Her current book traces the journey of *The Secret River*'s research and writing.

Anita Heiss is a member of the Wiradjuri nation of central New South Wales and is an author, poet, social commentator and cultural activist. Her published works include the historical novel *Who Am I? The Diary of Mary Talence, Sydney 1937,* the nonfiction text *Dhuuluu-Yala (To Talk Straight) – Publishing Aboriginal Literature* and the satirical social commentary *Sacred Cows*. Anita has performed her works in Australia, the United States, Canada, Spain, Austria and New Caledonia. She has also appeared on ABC TV's *Einstein Factor*, *Vulture*, *Critical Mass* and *Message Stick*. Anita is currently Deputy Director of the Department of Indigenous Studies at Macquarie University and she has a PhD in Communication and Media.

John Kinsella's most recent volumes of poetry include *Peripheral Light: Selected and New Poems* (FACP and WW Norton, 2003), *Doppler Effect* (Salt, 2004) and *The New Arcadia* (FACP and WW Norton, 2005). His memoir, *Fast, Loose Beginnings*, was published by Melbourne University Press in August 2006.

Christopher Kremmer's writing has been compared to the work of Joseph Conrad and Nobel laureate V. S. Naipaul. His bestselling book *The Carpet Wars*, a sweeping portrait of a swathe of Islamic countries including Afghanistan, was described as moving and lyrical by the *Times Literary Supplement*. Born in Sydney and educated at the University of Canberra, his books and short stories have won several awards, and have been shortlisted for the prestigious *Age* Book of the Year, the NSW Premier's Literary Awards and the *Courier-Mail* Book of the Year. *Bamboo Palace*, his account of the last days of the Lao monarchy, one of Asia's oldest, has been praised as a definitive work by scholars of Asian history. His latest book, *Inhaling the Mahatma*, published in 2006 by HarperCollins, charts India's emergence from Gandhian self-reliance into the globalised world of the twenty-first century.

David Leser is a multi-award-winning journalist and author of four books. He is currently writing for the *Australian Women's Weekly*. Over the past twenty-five years he has worked as a feature writer for the *Australian*, the *Bulletin*, *HQ* magazine, the *Sydney Morning Herald*, the Sunday *Age* and *Good Weekend* magazine. He has also served as a correspondent in the Middle East and Washington DC. He now lives in Byron Bay with his wife and two daughters and is a regular interviewer at the Byron Bay Writers Festival.

Melissa Lucashenko is a Murri woman who writes about black people and poor people in modern Australia. When she isn't working on novels and critical essays, Melissa works in the local Koori community to ensure she stays close to her roots. She also breeds Australian stockhorses to ensure there is no danger of her ever becoming rich.

Mungo MacCallum has worked as a political commentator, writer and broadcaster since 1965. He currently writes for the Byron Shire *Echo*.

His latest publications are *Australian Political Anecdotes* and *Run Johnny Run: The Story of the 2004 Election.*

Roger McDonald is the author of seven novels, the most recent being *The Ballad of Desmond Kale*, and two works of nonfiction, *Shearers' Motel* and *The Tree in Changing Light*. He lives in the Southern Tablelands of New South Wales. *The Slim Find* is taken from an unpublished collection of loosely interconnected long stories, as yet untitled, set in places resembling those where he grew up and has lived in various phases of his life.

Craig McGregor is a writer, journalist and academic who has lived in Byron Bay, on and off, since the 1960s. He has written two novels, a book of short stories, and several books analysing Australian society, politics and popular culture, including *Class in Australia*, *Profile of Australia* and *Australian Son: Inside Mark Latham*. He was formerly Emeritus Professor of Communication at the University of Technology, Sydney. He is married with four children.

Hilary McPhee AO, former publisher and Chair of the Australia Council, was the inaugural Vice-Chancellor's Fellow at the University of Melbourne until the end of 2005. She is a board member of Melbourne University Publishing, and helped establish the Writing Centre for Scholars and Researchers at Melbourne University. She is a member of the Malthouse's Artistic Council and a 'columnist' on Radio National's *Book Show*. As a founding board member of the political website New Matilda.com she works to promote a Human Rights Act for Australia.

Di Morrissey has published thirteen best-selling novels in the past thirteen years, making her Australia's best-selling and most popular woman novelist. She has written all her life, as a journalist, copywriter, screenwriter and novelist. Her novels are inspired by landscape and she is well respected for her thorough research. She is Patron of

Southern Cross University Whale Research Centre and sits on several boards. She has been based in Byron Bay for fifteen years and has a daughter, Dr Gabrielle Morrissey, and a son, Nicolas Morrissey. Her fourteenth novel is *The Valley* (to be published in November 2006).

Ruth Ostrow is one of Australia's leading Mind Body Soul writers, with her weekly columns in the *Australian* read by millions, and a host of best-selling books in the areas of sexuality, human relations, money and well-being. A former finance journalist in the 1980s with the *Financial Review*, then a radio broadcaster in the 1990s in the area of relationships, Ruth now focuses her speaking and writings on wellness, longevity, spirituality and work–life balance from her home in Byron Bay where she moved from Sydney at the end of the 1990s.

Dorothy Porter is best known for her four verse novels, including *The Monkey's Mask*, which was made into a film in 2001, and most recently *Wild Surmise*, which won the Premier's Award at the 2004 Adelaide Arts Festival. Her verse novels *What a Piece of Work* and *Wild Surmise* were both shortlisted for the Miles Franklin Award. She wrote the lyrics for the Paul Grabowsky/Katie Noonan jazz album *Before Time Could Change Us* which won the Aria Award for Best Jazz album in 2005.

Peter Singer is Ira W. DeCamp Professor of Bioethics in the University Center for Human Values at Princeton University, and Laureate Professor in the Centre for Applied Philosophy and Practical Ethics at the University of Melbourne. He first became well known internationally after the publication of *Animal Liberation*. His other books include: *Practical Ethics: How Are We to Live?*, *Rethinking Life and Death*, *The President of Good and Evil: The Ethics of George W. Bush* and, most recently, *How Are We to Eat: Why Our Food Choices Matter* (with Jim Mason).

Robyn Williams has presented the *Science Show* on ABC Radio National for thirty-one years. His recent novel, *2007: A True Story Waiting to Happen*, was published by Hodder. His next book is called *Unintelligent Design* and is to be published in August 2006 by Allen & Unwin. He is a visiting professor at the University of New South Wales and has just had a star named after him.

EDITORS

Marele Day is the author of the bestselling literary novel *Lambs of God* (1997), which was published to acclaim in Australia and overseas, and the Claudia Valentine mysteries, including *The Last Tango of Dolores Delgado* (1992), winner of the American Shamus Award. She is the editor of *How to Write Crime* (1996), which won the Ned Kelly Award. Her most recent book is a novelised biography, *Mrs Cook: The Real and Imagined Life of the Captain's Wife* (2002). Marele lives on the north coast of New South Wales and is a frequent guest at the Byron Bay Writers Festival.

Susan Bradley Smith was born in Australia in 1963. Having lived much of her adult life in England, she now lives on the north coast of New South Wales with her husband and three children. A historian by training, she has taught literature, drama and creative writing as well as history in UK and Australian universities, and has published widely in these areas. Her memoir, *Friday Forever*, and a collection of poems, *Marmalade Exile*, will be published in 2006. She is currently writing a biography of Clementine Churchill.

Fay Knight is a freelance journalist and author of *Byron Bay Beauty* (Pan Macmillan, 2002). She is a committee member of the Northern Rivers Writers' Centre and has edited two members' anthologies.

ACKNOWLEDGMENTS

Thea Astley's 'Why I Wrote a Short Story called "Diesel Epiphany"' was first published in *Meanjin* 45, 2 (1986) and in 1987 was published by UQP in *Collected Stories: Thea Astley*.

Jean Bedford's story 'The Woman on the Train' was commissioned for *The 21st Century Tarot Deck*, compiled by George Papaellinas, Helen Addison-Smith, Justin Clemens & Thomas Deverall, as a writer's response to The Empress card.

John Carroll's 'Universal Rights – Singular Culture' was published in the Saturday *Australian* in September 2005.

'Helen Garner and the Agony of Writing' is reprinted from an article published in the *Australian Women's Weekly* and then republished in *Dames and Divas: 21 Remarkable Women* by David Leser and published by Park Street Press.

Peter Goldsworthy's 'Travels with My Inner Toad' was first published in the *Sydney Morning Herald*, Good Weekend, 12 November 2005.

John Kinsella's poem 'Line Breaks and Back Drafts' was published in *poetry review* in the United Kingdom.

Ruth Ostrow's short story 'The Violin' is an extract from *Sacred & Naked* by Ruth Ostrow, published by Hardie Grant books.

Dorothy Porter's poem 'Numbers' was first published in a limited edition chapbook, *Poems January–August 2004* by Vagabond Press, 2004.

ENDNOTES

Anita Heiss: Aboriginal Writers on the Significance of Space, Sense of Place and Connection to Country

1. Samuel Wagan Watson, 'Recipe for Metropolis Brisbane', in 'Stories Without End', *Southerly*, vol. 62, no. 2, 2002, p. 44.
2. Brenda Palma, 'Sydney Real Estate For Sale', in *Life in Gadigal Country*, ed. Anita Heiss, Gadigal Information Services, Sydney, 2001, p. 85.
3. Brenda L. Croft, 'Wuganmagulya (Farm Cove)', in *Life in Gadigal Country*, op. cit., pp. 28–29.
4. Samuel Wagan Watson, 'Jaded Olympic Moments', in *Smoke Encrypted Whispers*, UQP, St Lucia, 2004, p. 126.
5. ibid., p. 104.
6. Molly Mallett, *My Past – Their Future: Stories from Cape Barren Island*, Blubber Head Press, Sandy Bay, 2001, p. 46.
7. Charlotte Phillips, in *Papunya School Book of Country and History*, Allen & Unwin, East Melbourne, 2001, p. 4.
8. Magdelene Williams, *Ngay jannijirr ngank: This Is My Word*, ed. Pat Torres, Magabala Books, Broome, 1999, pp. 53–55.
9. Williams, ibid., 'Author's Note'.
10. Rita Huggins, *Aunty Rita*, Aboriginal Studies Press, ACT, 1994.
11. Terri Janke, http://www.abc.net.au/message/blackarts/review/s1133205.htm.

12. Kerry Reed-Gilbert, *Black Woman, Black Life*, Wakefield Press, Kent Town, SA, 1996, p. 63.
13. Kerry Reed-Gilbert, 'Uluru Dreamin' 1', in *Talkin' About Country*, Kuracca Communications, ACT, 1999.
14. Jennifer Martiniello, 'Uluru by Champagne', in *The Imprint of Infinity*, Tidbinbilla Press, ACT, 1999.

John Kinsella: Line Breaks and Back-Draft
1. http://www.johnkinsella.org/interviews/adamson.html
2. http://support.microsoft.com/default.aspx?scid=kb;EN-US;q287816
3. http://jacketmagazine.com/06/kins.html
4. *Australian Book Review*, November 2000, Issue 226.

John Carroll: Universal Rights – Singular Culture
1. Samuel Huntington, *The Clash of Civilizations and the Remaking of World Order*, Simon & Schuster, New York, 1996. The thesis was first put in an essay in 1993. Huntington also argued that, in the short to medium term, Islam would violently clash with most of the other civilisations. September 11 seemed to vindicate the thesis.
2. I have attempted to spell out these archetypes, as nine stories fundamental to the West, in the book *The Western Dreaming* (HarperCollins, Sydney, 2001).
3. Bernard Lewis, *What Went Wrong? The Clash between Modernity and Islam in the Middle East*, Weidenfeld & Nicolson, London, 2002.
4. Rohan Gunaratna provides an authoritative history of Al Qaeda, and the beliefs and organisational structure of Osama bin Laden, in *Inside Al Qaeda* (Scribe, Melbourne, 2002).
5. Paul Berman, *Terror and Liberalism*, Norton, New York, 2003, pp. 60–102.
6. The formative modern expression of this view is that of the Enlightenment's one great philosopher, Immanuel Kant. In his

Critique of Practical Reason, published in 1788, Kant stipulated the moral law as universal, and laid down the principles according to which the free and rational modern individual should obey that law.
7. I have previously sought to interpret September 11 in terms of its cultural challenge to the West, in *Terror: A Meditation on the Meaning of September 11* (Scribe, Melbourne, 2002). That short book reads the attack on New York through Western works, from Conrad's *Heart of Darkness* to the recent film *Fight Club*.

Alison Broinowski: This is the way the world ends

1. Bill Moyers, 'Welcome to Doomsday', *New York Review of Books*, 24 March 2005, pp. 8–10.
2. Marion Maddox, 'What should be the place of religion in Australian politics?', *Peace Yearbook*, People for Nuclear Disarmament NSW, 2005.
3. Quoted by Don Watson, 'A Jekyll-and-Hyde just waiting in the wings', *Sydney Morning Herald*, 26 August 2005, p. 13.
4. Quoted by Robyn Williams, 'Of Gods and humankind', *Peace Yearbook*, People for Nuclear Disarmament NSW, 2005.
5. Quoted from literature in the bookshop attached to Sheikh Mohammed Omran's Melbourne prayer room (*Australian*, 22 August 2005, p. 9).
6. V. S. Naipaul, quoted by Rachel Donadio, 'At home with the irascible prophet', *Weekend Australian*, 20–21 August 2005, pp. 8–9.
7. Quoted in *The American Conservative*, 18 July 2005. Robert Pape, *Dying to Win: The Strategic Logic of Suicide Terrorism*, Scribe, Melbourne, 2005.
8. George Monbiot, 'Sounds of war echo in calls to patriotism', *Sydney Morning Herald*, 11 August 2005, p. 13.
9. John Stone, 'The case for assimilation', *Australian*, 15 August 2005.

10. Imre Saluzinsky, 'Get to know your enemy', *Weekend Australian*, 13–14 August 2005, p. R40.
11. John Deutch, Institute Professor, Massachusetts Institute of Technology, 'Iraq', Phi Beta Kappa Oration, 7 June 2005, in *Harvard Magazine*, 2005.
12. Robert F. Kennedy Jr, *Crimes Against Nature: How George W. Bush and His Corporate Pals Are Plundering Our Country and Hijacking Our Democracy*, HarperCollins, New York, 2005.
13. Tim Flannery, 'Endgame', *New York Review of Books*, 11 August 2005, pp. 26–29.
14. Jean-Marie Guehenno, UN Director of Peacekeeping Operations, *The End of the Nation-State*, University of Minnesota Press, 1995, p. 139, quoted by Tony Judt, 'Europe vs. America', *New York Review of Books*, 10 February 2005, pp. 37–41.